T0313261

The 2008 crisis came close to toppling the global financial system. We continue to live with its iniquitous consequences today. *Commodity* takes a step back from the day-to-day oscillations in financial markets to ask how a financialised logic came to dominate and shape the contemporary world economy. This book is essential reading for academics, students and the general reader who wish to better understand how financial capitalism rose to ascendance – and how it might be challenged through an ambitious programme of transnational tax reform.

Scott Lavery, University of Sheffield, UK

Commodity

The 21st century marks a watershed in the history of the human economic condition. Income and wealth inequalities are now greater than ever before – and their role in the global financial crisis is one of the burning issues of today.

Commodity looks at the great financial crisis from an entirely original perspective – that of the global commodity system as a newly operational totality. In the 19th century, the commodity system as defined by Karl Marx was limited to a few regions and embraced only the labour and capital capacities and their outputs. By the end of the 20th century, it encompassed the entire planet and embraced government capacity as well as private capacities, financial securities and material goods and services. This book shows how the financial crisis and its causes can only properly be understood as a result of this vast, unprecedented extension of the commodity system – a system which benefits the rich. The author makes the watertight case that it is only through the creation of a global tax authority – to coordinate national tax regimes and to implement a tax on global wealth – that we can avoid another crisis and create a fairer and more equitable world.

Addressing a broad range of themes, *Commodity* offers a new perspective which will be of interest to political economists as well as researchers specialising in other related fields of social enquiry. Written in a clear and engaging way, the book's concise nature also makes it accessible for the non-specialist reader, and it will especially appeal to all those who want a more just society.

Photis Lysandrou is a research professor in the Department of International Politics at City University Political Economy Research Centre (CITYPERC), UK. Previously he has taught economics at City University, Greenwich University and at London Metropolitan University, where he was Lead Professor in Economics.

Routledge Frontiers of Political Economy

For more information about this series, please visit: www.routledge.
com/books/series/SE0345

Commodity
The Global Commodity System
in the 21st Century

Photis Lysandrou

Routledge
Taylor & Francis Group

LONDON AND NEW YORK

First published 2019
by Routledge
2 Park Square, Milton Park, Abingdon, Oxon OX14 4RN

and by Routledge
52 Vanderbilt Avenue, New York, NY 10017

Routledge is an imprint of the Taylor & Francis Group, an informa business

© 2019 Photis Lysandrou

British Library Cataloguing-in-Publication Data
A catalogue record for this book is available from the British Library

Library of Congress Cataloging-in-Publication Data
A catalog record has been requested for this book

ISBN: 978-1-138-33860-9 (hbk)
ISBN: 978-0-429-44159-2 (ebk)

Typeset in Times New Roman
by codeMantra

For Yvonne

Contents

Acknowledgements

My sincere thanks to Andy Humphries, Economics Editor at Routledge, for his initiative and assistance in helping to bring this book to publication. I also thank Anna Cuthbert and her production team at Routledge and Jeanine Furino and her project team at codeMantra for the proficiency with which this book was produced. I thank two reviewers for their comments on an earlier draft of this work and for their helpful suggestions. I thank Bob Morgan for his positive response to the very first draft of the whole text. Finally, for their warm support and encouragement during the writing of this work, I thank members of my family, notably my brother Lysandros, my daughter Marika and, above all, my wife Yvonne.

Preface

The purpose of this short book is to provide a generalising insight into the contemporary global economic condition. To this end, it deploys an analytical framework whose basic unit of analysis is the commodity principle as defined by Marx. During the course of Marx's lifetime, that principle was only dominant in a few regions, and even then, it only encompassed the private capacities of capital and labour power and their material outputs. By the end of the 20th century, the commodity principle had been not only further stretched to encompass virtually the entire surface of the planet but also further deepened to cover the public capacity to govern, in addition to private capacities, and financial securities, in addition to material goods and services. Thus, the contemporary global economic condition is viewed from the standpoint of this newly emergent global commodity system. To facilitate the flow of discussion, the book is divided into five parts that respectively deal with the structure, genesis, operation, crisis and control of the global commodity system. Finally, in keeping with the book's concise content and structure, endnotes are kept to a minimum and serve primarily to reference the published papers where certain arguments presented in the text were first developed.

The wealth of those societies in which the capitalist mode of production prevails, presents itself as "an immense accumulation of commodities, its unit being a single commodity". Our investigation must therefore begin with the analysis of a single commodity.

(Karl Marx, Das Kapital, 1867)

1 Structure

1.1

There are about 200 independent nation states in the world, and almost all of them are integrated into the global market economy. There are hundreds of thousands of large organisations in the world, the great majority of which have a market-related function. Finally, there are some seven billion people occupying the planet, and although not all of them are involved in the global division of labour, a substantial number do have some involvement. In what follows, the focus of attention will be on the linkages binding together the countries, organisations and individuals that play a role in the global economy. These linkages have been the object of investigation of countless studies, but what is unusual about the present study is its use of a 'two-space' perspective, one which starts from the proposition that all of the aforementioned entities simultaneously inhabit a 'physical' space where they relate to each other in their differentiated forms as countries, organisations and individuals and a 'commodity' space where they relate to each other in their homogenised forms as providers of commodities.[1] The rationale for deploying such a perspective is that it enables one to gain certain insights into the contemporary human condition that cannot otherwise be gained. In elaborating on this claim, we begin by sketching out the present-day structure of the global commodity system.[2]

1.2

A commodity is a social category in the sense that any entity that has a use value can be classified as a commodity if its exchange value is determined against socially established standards rather than by private negotiation.[3] The most elementary types of entity that qualify as commodities, and which form the material base on which all other commodities ultimately rest, are goods and services. Two conditions are required for this particular qualification to be met. The first is that individuals are organised in a division of labour such that they typically produce for each other rather than for self-subsistence. The second concerns the scale of the division of labour system. If the system is limited to a small community of individuals, it follows that goods and services need not become commodities given that it is possible for the community to exchange outputs on terms that can be negotiated on an associative basis. On the contrary, if the scale of interdependent relations between specialised individuals exceeds a minimum threshold such that it becomes impossible for them to know each other's personal needs and thus to produce to order and negotiate exchange terms accordingly, it then becomes generally necessary for these individuals to produce goods and services to socially established standards of production and provision and to accept the exchange ratios as determined by the prevailing standards. Most of the goods and services traded in the world today are commodities as defined earlier. There is a further point. While a sizeable proportion of these goods and services continue to be produced and traded according to regional or country standards, the majority are commodities in the global sense in that in their case production and pricing standards have become more or less harmonised at the global level.[4]

A commodity system presupposes the institution of money. In physical space, this institution has emerged to help overcome the various costs of barter exchange: thus the measure of value function helps to overcome the problem of negotiating terms of trade by providing a yardstick against which physically heterogeneous entities can be rendered commensurable; the medium of exchange function makes redundant the need to satisfy the mutual coincidence of wants criterion by splitting sales and purchases into two separate, self-contained acts; the store of value function, finally, helps to support the medium of exchange function by permitting the storage of purchasing power between the acts of sale and purchase. In commodity space, the same three functions of money are crucial to the reconciliation between the social rule of price determination on the one hand and the private mode of price formation on the other.[5] In a social division of labour, prices must accord with a determinate set of ratios for both qualitative and quantitative reasons, where the former, as already observed, denotes the need for commodities to conform to socially sanctioned production standards and where the latter denotes the need for the amount of any given type of commodity that is supplied to match an equivalent amount of demand for it. As there is no central price-setting authority in a commodity exchange system, commodity prices can only converge to a set of rule governed ratios through the decentralised process of price formation based on the three functions of money: through its use as measure of value, agents can assign prices to their commodities (money in this function facilitates price assignment); through the offers or non-offers of money as a medium of exchange, privately assigned prices are either validated or falsified (money in this function facilitates price realisation); while the use of money as a store of value enables agents to bridge the gaps between sales and purchases (money in this function helps to sustain the continuity of a decentralised price formation process). Given that most commodities produced in the world today conform to globally harmonised standards of production, logic dictates that there should exist a world money that fulfils all three of the aforementioned functions. As there is no such money in practice, the alternative solution is for a few national currencies to duplicate their functions at the international level, with the exchange rates of the remaining national currencies being tied to one or other of these internationally used currencies.[6]

Just as goods and services are mapped into price space as commodities, so also are the human capacities for producing these material outputs. There are three types of capacity, two private and one public. The commodity principle is expanded to include labour power when the majority of individuals are separated from their means of production and thus from their means of subsistence and, as a result, are compelled to sell their capacity for labour for a money wage. The coexistence of a property-owning class alongside the class of propertyless agents implies that the labour power capacity is confronted by an opposing capital capacity, that of deploying privately owned means of production in conjunction with labour power to produce goods and services for a profit. The fact that capacities are commodities means that the decentralised, money-based process of price formation described earlier is also one that involves the validation or falsification of profits and wages. Thus, the validation of prices of particular goods or services that include profit markups informs producers that their capital has been deployed according to both a qualitative standard of production and a quantitative rule of allocation, while the converse is the case with the falsification of these prices consequent on non-offers to buy. Wages are subject to two different types of price formation process, one inside the confines of the firm through the associative relation with the owner of capital and the other inside the wider marketplace through the impersonal exchange relation; either way, the validation of privately assigned wages indicates that the labour powers offered meet required skill levels as well as being offered in the right quantities, while the converse is the case with the falsification of assigned wages consequent on non-offers of money.

The public capacity of government can be defined in terms of a determinate relationship between public expenditure, the financial means of executing government objectives, and taxes as the principal form of income commanded by governments. This dual aspect of government finance explains why the growth in the scale of its capacity to govern is necessarily interdependent with the growth of the domestic economy as a whole. Since goods, labour and capital form the three major sources of tax revenue, it follows that the expansion in the role of government is itself contingent on that of production and exchange activities in general. Conversely, government spending contributes to the growth of a domestic economy, both in an indirect sense insofar as some of this spending is used to maintain a regulatory framework without which the continuity of production and exchange is impossible, and in a direct sense insofar as a proportion of this spending is for the provision of certain goods and services that are required by an economic system but which would not be furnished at all, or not furnished in the quantity and with the efficiency required, by the private sector. As with the private capacities of capital and labour, the government capacity becomes commoditised at the point where its deployment is monitored and constrained against socially sanctioned standards of behaviour. The difference is that where such standards covering private capacities can exist at both a local and a global level, the same is not true of the public capacity. Given that a national government is sovereign in a domestic economy, there is no comparable domestic entity against which its economic and social policies can be judged. Only in a global context, where there are many national governments but also where none are sovereign, can the very idea of a uniform standard for comparing the behaviour and activities of governments assume operational significance.

One of the principal reasons why behavioural standards for governments coexist alongside those for private corporations is so that the risk on government bonds can be quantified and factored into their prices in the same way that is done for corporate bonds and equities. This point brings us to the final major category of commodities, namely, financial securities. In its complete form, a global commodity system constitutes a three-tiered system: the human capacities for activity, the material goods and services that are the realised outcomes of this activity, and the debt and equity securities that are the tradable claims on the future expected outcomes of corporate and government activity. The corporations and governments issuing securities never see them as commodities in their own right but only as a means of financing the production of commodities. It is different with large institutional investors, such as pension funds, mutual funds and insurance companies, which are today the predominant types of security holders. For these investors, securities constitute 'investables', assets whose use values are to serve as stores of value into which clients' money can be poured and from which money can be withdrawn to repay clients.[7] In principle, other assets such as real estate, gold and other natural commodities can also be used as value containers. However, the physical constraints on the supplies of these assets, combined with certain disadvantageous attributes and most notably a lack of liquidity, defined here as ease of trading with minimal impact on price, mean that institutional investors have to depend on financial securities as the major type of investable asset. It is this dependence that compels institutional investors to view corporations and governments as 'dual commodity providers', organisations whose function is to supply the debt and equity securities that are required for asset management needs just as it is to supply the material goods and services that are required for consumption or production needs.[8]

There are two preconditions for the commoditisation of securities to be possible. The first is that the activity of governments and private corporations must be tied to prevailing production and service provision standards for the obvious reason that without some demonstrable commitment to these standards on the part of security-issuing organisations, there can be no reasonable guarantee of the size and stability of the income flows against which claims are made. While necessary to the commoditisation of securities, this first precondition is not sufficient. Corporations can excel in production but still decide not to distribute cash to investors for one reason or another. Similarly, governments can excel in service provision and generate tax revenues accordingly but still give a low priority to the payment of interest on bonds. This brings us to the second precondition for the commoditisation of securities, which is the need to tie the various organisations issuing them to governance standards. Broadly defined, the governance of an organisation concerns the way in which it conducts its affairs so as to meet the different priorities of its various stakeholders. From the standpoint of investors, the question of corporate or public sector governance essentially boils down to the level of priority given to their interests as shareholders or bondholders: high priority means that there is a reasonably good guarantee that cash will be returned to them in the required amounts and at the required intervals, whereas a low priority means that there is no guarantee that cash will be returned. Given that equities pay dividends at the discretion of corporate managers, a high ranking of shareholders' interests in the ordering of a corporation's priorities is absolutely essential to the commoditisation of equity securities. At the same time, although the payment of interests on bonds is fixed by law, good governance as defined here is also a crucial condition for the commoditisation of debt securities inasmuch as any organisation issuing them can still rank its priorities in a way that can disrupt, or even negate, any contractually agreed stream of interest payments.

It is at the point where financial securities become commodities in the sense described earlier that the commodity system must occupy its own distinct space. As long as commodity systems simply comprised capacities and their material outputs, the interactions between the different parts of those systems could still place within physical space. However, for the commodity principle to be deepened to the point where it can also encompass financial securities, at that point, the interactions between the different component parts of a commodity system have to take place within their own space, a space that is distinct from physical space in that it is an entirely social construction that owes nothing to nature. The crux of the matter is the indispensability of the commodity principle to the store of value function of financial securities. Strip goods and services of their commodity attributes, and their materiality, or use value properties, continue to exist independently of whether they are priced and exchanged against socially established production standards. Similarly, strip human capacities for activity of their commodity attributes, and these capacities still have a material existence independently of whether the outcomes of these activities are subject to social standards. By contrast, the consequences of any relaxation of the commodity principle for financial securities are very different. Relax the pressures forcing the deployment of capacities and the pricing of material outputs against social standards, and the ability of financial securities to serve as value containers is severely diminished, if not lost altogether. This may not be a problem for corporations and governments because for them it is only the flow dimension of securities that really matters: they raise funds through the issuance of securities on the promise to repay the funds at some future date, and in the meantime, they use the funds for investment purposes. It is a problem, however, for institutional investors who need to be concerned as much with the stock or quantity dimension of securities as with their flow dimension: they give sums of money when purchasing securities in the expectation of being repaid at some future date, but in the meantime, they need to use these securities as value containers. As securities have no intrinsic value, their value storage property is determined entirely by the degree to which their prices are held firm and thus made tangible, a condition that depends in turn on the degree to which the security issuing organisations are made to conform with production standards such that ensure their ability to return cash and with governance standards such that ensure their readiness to return cash.

In sum, it is because the actions of institutional investors are key to the completion of the commodity system that they at the same time help us understand why that system exists in a socially constructed space that is distinct from physical space. All groups of agents play some role or other in the commoditisation of goods and services through helping to establish the production standards against which these are priced and traded. However, it is institutional investors, by virtue of the exigencies of their asset management function, who are the principal agents through which governance standards become established alongside production standards, thereby making it possible for financial securities to acquire a solidity that they cannot have in physical space. This is not all. In pushing for the creation of conditions such as can allow financial securities to circulate as commodities in their own right, the actions of institutional investors help us to understand not only how the commodity system comes to occupy a socially constructed space that parallels physical space but also how these two spaces then continue to coexist in relations both of mutual dependence and of mutual antithesis. In expanding on this argument, it is first explained why the two spaces are mutually antithetical.

1.3

Physical space is complex because its major distinguishing feature is one of heterogeneity. Commodity space by contrast is much simpler because the major distinguishing feature here is one of homogeneity. This distinction is immediately apparent in respect of individual agents. In physical space individuals can be grouped together according to any number of classifications, including gender, social status, specialisation and position in the division of labour and so on, but it is the feature of difference and heterogeneity that prevails in that even individuals who share a similar social status or perform similar tasks can still differ appreciably in terms of character, temperament and ability. Conversely, although there is an element of heterogeneity in commodity space, in that individual agents can be grouped together according to the type of capacity for activity that they each have, it is the homogeneity feature that prevails here. This is because in commodity space abstraction is made from the personalities of the individuals who possess particular capacities and because there are in any case only three types of human capacity, the private capacities of capital and labour power and the public capacity of government.

Aggregating upwards, we find that the difference in the heterogeneity-homogeneity ordering across the two spaces applies as much to organisations as to the individuals comprising them. Take physical space. There is a degree of homogeneity here in that all private business corporations operate to a profit motive while government institutions typically operate to a non-profit principle. Heterogeneity prevails in this space, however, in that it is the functional differences separating business corporations and their corresponding forms of fee income that are paramount. Thus, industrial corporations produce material goods for industrial profit; banks hire out the services of money as a medium of exchange in return for an interest charge; rental firms hire out property, machinery or consumer durables such as cars and charge rent. By contrast, it is the homogeneity property that prevails in commodity space, in that here all private firms, whatever their specific business activity and whatever their specific form of income generation, exist merely as commodity clusters, combinations of the human capacities of capital and labour power on the one hand with non-human inputs on the other. This homogeneity property extends also to government organisations in that while these substantively differ from business organisations in physical space because of their difference in function, in commodity space they too appear merely as commodity clusters, albeit that it is the government capacity that here substitutes for the capital capacity in combining with labour power and non-human inputs to produce a stream of public services.

What has been said here also applies to securities, financial claims on the future income streams generated by corporations and governments. In physical space, securities share a certain similarity in that they all represent market-based forms of finance, financial claims in the form of tradable instruments, as opposed to bank-based forms of finance, financial claims in the form of a credit relation between known counterparties. However, it is the different functions that separate types of securities that are paramount in physical space because of the importance of these functions to the organisations issuing the securities. Thus, equities as ownership entitlements allow corporations to share the risk of enterprise with investors albeit at the cost of a certain dilution of the benefits of ownership. By contrast, bonds as credit instruments allow corporations to raise funds without dilution of ownership but have as their downside the possibility that they can force corporations into default. In commodity space, it is the homogeneity feature of financial securities that is paramount: here they represent a distinct class of investable assets that differ from other asset classes in that they have no intrinsic value and thus can only fulfil a value storage function when security issuing organisations are tied to certain production and governance standards that determine their propensity to return cash to investors. The differences between securities come into play within this broader context of their common feature as tradable claims on future income streams: namely, their different combinations of risk and return. Thus corporate equities that pay dividends on discretion carry on average higher risk-return ratios than do corporate bonds that pay interest by law, while the latter in turn generally carry higher risk-return ratios than do government bonds, because the interest that corporations pay on bonds is financed out of their profits that vary more considerably over the business cycle than do the tax revenues that are the principal sources of revenue for the interest paid by governments on their bonds.

It is in relation to countries that the mutual antithesis of physical and commodity spaces finds expression on the grandest scale. In physical space, countries are containers of people: what is paramount here are the local rules, institutions, customs and traditions that provide a stable and socially cohesive environment where peoples' capacities for activity can be deployed on a regular basis. In commodity space, countries are commodity masses, agglomerations of commodity clusters: what is paramount here are the global standards for the deployment and pricing of capacities, for the production and pricing of material outputs and for the issuance and pricing of the financial securities that lay claim to future outputs. In physical space governments are sovereign. It is they who lay down and enforce the various laws, rules and regulations that guide or constrain the conduct and behaviour of all citizens living and working within the particular government's jurisdiction. In short, it is governments that give operational meaning not only to the idea of nationhood but also to the reality of nations as physically bordered entities. In commodity space, governments are not sovereign. In this space government organisations simply represent commodity clusters just like other clusters in which the deployment of the public capacity to govern is subject to globally sanctioned standards just as are private capacities. This observation brings us to the difference between internationalism and globalism. In physical space it is the bordered nation state that is the foundational unit. There are many and varied types of cross-border interconnections within and across business corporations and government organisations that are maintained by various negotiated agreements, treaties and so on; that said, internationalism in physical space is essentially nothing other than an extrapolation of the basic national unit. In commodity space, everything is the other way around. It is the globally established behavioural standards and pricing rules that determine the respective size of countries as commodity masses and the position that these masses occupy within global commodity space. In short, commodity space globalisation is essentially nothing other than physical space internationalisation turned inside out.

It is here that institutional asset managers re-enter the picture, in that they are the one group of agents that actually view the world from an inverted commodity standpoint. While all other groups of agents that participate in the global market economy effectively occupy a second space parallel to physical space, none of them have to actually see this second space and conduct their activities accordingly. Individual workers do not typically view themselves in the abstract as owners of a particular capacity that enables them to occupy a particular position or cell in the global commodity matrix. Their labour power may be mapped into commodity space, but what they only see, and only need to see, is the concrete, physical reality around them, the reality of the local community where they live, work and socialise with other people. The same is true of corporations. These may exist in commodity space as clusters of human capacities and non-human inputs, but what anyone managing a manufacturing firm or a commercial bank has to prioritise if they are to successfully carry out their management function is the physical reality of the environment in which they are located and the physical attributes, characteristics, positions etc. of the individuals that they employ or lend money to and so on. Large corporations typically operate across many countries and regions, but even here each of their local subsidiaries or branches must take into account the local customs, cultural values and codes of conduct when conducting their operations. Finally, the same is also true of government officials in that they can only effectively fulfil their public service function by speaking the language of the local populace, by respecting their customs, values and traditions, by sharing, or appearing to share, their anxieties and concerns, by participating in their celebrations and ceremonies and so on.

With institutional investors everything is the complete opposite. They live and operate in physical space, as do other individuals and as does every other business organisation, but their very function as asset managers forces them to take a commodity perspective on the world. In order to reach a particular risk-reward target, institutional investors must diversify not only within but also across equity and bond portfolios This need for wide diversification entails a consequent need to abstract from many of the individual characteristics and peculiarities that separate corporations and governments in favour of a view that places these organisations on a par as clusters of capacities capable of producing a given stream of outputs and thus capable of supporting a given stock of securities, the only differences needing to be taken into consideration in this homogenising perspective being those that impact on the risk quality of the securities. This same homogenising view also extends to countries. The fact that institutional investors are typically required to diversify not only across domestic portfolios but also across foreign portfolios means that they must abstract from the peculiarities of language, culture, traditions etc. that separate countries as distinct containers of people, in favour of a homogenising perspective that places countries on a commensurable par as agglomerations of human capacities and non-human resources, the only differences needing to be taken into consideration being those that impact on the risk quality of the securities issued by the corporations and governments belonging to these countries.

1.4

Physical and commodity spaces are not only mutually antithetical but also mutually dependent. The reasons behind commodity space's dependence on physical space are straightforward. As financial securities are nothing other than claims on the future incomes of corporations and governments, they can have no meaningful existence outside of these organisations' ability to generate these incomes by means of the continuous production of material commodities, a continuity that in turn requires these organisations to be firmly grounded in physical space localities due to a combination of factors that broadly divide into two categories: the political and the social. The political factors pertain to social stability: the continuity of production is more easily maintained in a structured and bordered environment in which the activities of individuals and organisations are subject to the rule of law. The social factors pertain to social community: individual agents are not mechanical units but human beings that need to group together in communities where they relate to each other not only as producers and consumers or as employers and employees but also as individuals sharing a common language, as citizens sharing common values and customs, as voters sharing common rights and responsibilities and so on. The upshot of all this is that institutional investors have to make compromises in the demands they make of security issuing organisations: investors may need these organisations to conform to such standards as can allow for the comparison and pricing of securities and as can uphold their value storage property, but conformity cannot be pushed to the point where it begins to negate the various physical space factors that sustain the continuity of production.

The reasons behind the reverse line of dependence running from physical space to commodity space basically come down to the financing needs of the corporations and governments that are the major suppliers of goods and services in any modern market economy. Three points can be made in this regard to these needs. The first is that there are limits to how much these organisations can finance their production or service provision activities out of their current incomes: when these limits are reached, organisations are forced to supplement their funding needs by resorting to external forms of finance. The second point is that there are limits as to how much these organisations can raise through non-security market sources of finance, such as bank loans in the case of corporations and increased issuance of domestic money in the case of governments: when these limits are reached, organisations are forced to depend on security market sources of finance. The final point is that security market dependence can be of two forms: dependence that is small or large but temporary in nature and dependence that is both large in scale and permanent. Security market dependence of the first form does not require any special type of investor on the buy side of the market. The final end-suppliers of funds could, for example, simply be household investors who choose to allocate some of their savings to financial securities rather than hold them with banks. By contrast, the second form of security market dependence does require a special type of investor on the buy side of the market, namely, institutional asset managers such as insurance companies and pension funds that have liabilities on a scale and of a duration that can match the fundraising needs of the security issuing organisations.

It is precisely this scale and duration of institutional asset managers' liabilities that requires them to treat securities as investables, assets with value storage capacities of a determinate size that can be maintained over determinate stretches of time. Furthermore, it is precisely this requirement that, as a condition for its fulfilment, necessitates the existence of a distinct, socially constructed space where securities can have a meaningful existence as value containers, namely, commodity space. In physical space, securities are mere air, promises by those raising funds to return funds. Only in commodity space can securities assume a quantitative dimension because of the supporting infrastructure of social institutions, constraints and obligations. The explanation bears repeating: as financial securities have no material substance, their value storage capacities are determined exclusively by their prices; as these prices are nothing other than the present, discounted values of expected future returns, it follows that their tangibility, the reliability with which they constitute specified quantities of value, depends on the extent to which there is a reasonable guarantee that the promised streams of returns will actually materialise; finally, such a guarantee can only be assured when security issuers comply with socially sanctioned production and governance standards that respectively determine their ability and willingness to return cash to investors. The upshot here is that security issuing corporations and governments need to make compromises in the extent to which they resist financial market constraints: they need some freedom from these constraints in order to give themselves room to exercise their production or service provision function, but this freedom cannot be pushed to the point where it undermines the value storage property of securities and thus their use value to institutional investors.

1.5

To summarise, all agents that have a role in the global economy effectively occupy two parallel spaces, a physical space where they deploy their capacities for activity and a commodity space where their capacities are priced against social standards as are their material outputs and as are the financial securities that lay claim to these outputs. The two spaces are distinct because they are mutually dependent. If the line of dependence ran just one way, from commodity space to physical space, there would be no need for the former to exist as a structured space in its own right. On the contrary, it is because many of the major producers of material goods and services rely on the issuance of financial securities to maintain the continuity of their production, and it is because institutional investors can only absorb these securities on the scale required by obliging issuers to conform to a system of social standards and behavioural constraints that a fully fledged commodity space comes into existence. At the same time, it is because it is through the initiatives of institutional investors that a commodity space emerges as a distinct structured space in its own right that it then coexists with physical space, as much in a relation of mutual antithesis as in one of mutual dependence: the two spaces lock

together as the inverted opposites of each other. The production functions of corporations and governments may require them to respect
the heterogeneity of the physical space localities in which they operate,
but in being dependent on the securities markets to help finance the
continuity of their production or service provision, they are in effect
dependent on investors whose asset management function compels
them to view the world from a homogenising, global commodity space
perspective and to operate accordingly.

Notes

1 The two-space perspective used here was first introduced in Lysandrou
   and Lysandrou (2003).
2 See Lysandrou (2005) for a first sketch of the global commodity system's
   structure.
3 Following Marx, 'commodity' is here defined in a way that is both more
   exclusive and more inclusive than is usual: the former in that only entities
   that are priced and traded according to social standards are classified as
   commodities, and the latter in that certain entities other than material
   outputs can also be classified as commodities. While this particular
   coincidence with Marx may not cause controversy, the situation is likely
   to be different as regards the claim made in the preface to this work that
   the analytical framework as developed here is in line with that of Marx.
   Going by the generally held assumption that Marx's overarching framework is based on a 'labour theory of value', an assumption that links in
   with the view that Marx's starting point is with the aggregative category
   of 'class', it would seem that much of what is said in this present work
   breaks with Marx. However, this conventional assumption is wrong.
   Class and class exploitation are certainly connected with the commodity, but the connection proposed by Marx runs in a direction that begins
   with a reductionist, disaggregated standpoint before proceeding to an
   aggregative class position. In his final work on political economy, 'Notes
   on Wagner' written in 1879 (but only first published in English in 1976,
   which might explain why it is still largely unknown), Marx states:

   > 'Another thing Mr Wagner forgets is that neither "value" nor "exchange
   > value" are subjects in my work, but rather the *commodity*' (Marx, 1976,
   > p. 204) ....According to Mr Wagner, *use value* and *exchange value* are
   > to be derived at once from the *concept of value*, not as with me, from a
   > *concretum, the commodity.*
   >
   > (Marx, 1976, p. 208)

   In beginning with a concretum, the commodity, Marx in effect begins
   with a single representative individual, one viewed not subjectively, as a
   rational choice maximising agent as in mainstream neoclassical theories,
   but objectively, as a seller of commodities, entities that are priced and
   traded against social standards. In support of this interpretation, consider
   this further comment by Marx:

> In the first place, I do not proceed on the basis of 'concepts' hence also not from the 'value-concept', and I do not have the task of 'dividing' it up in any way, for that reason. What I proceed from is the simplest social form in which the product of labour in contemporary society manifests itself, and this is as 'commodity'.
>
> (Marx, 1976, p. 214)

In the first part of Volume 1 of *Capital*, only the material products of labour qualify as commodities in the aforementioned sense. Thereafter, Marx expands the commodity category to include the private capacities of labour power and capital and, in so doing, aggregates representative individuals into two representative classes. That is where he stopped. Marx did not proceed further with this commodity expansion because he could not do so given the circumstances of his time. It is only on the basis of recent developments that one can see how the commodity principle as first defined by Marx has been expanded to encompass the public capacity of government in addition to the private capacities and financial securities in addition to material goods and services.

4 See Lysandrou (2005) for further discussion and references.
5 See Lysandrou (1987, 1990) for an early account of money's role in price formation.
6 For further discussion of this point, see Karltenbrunner and Lysandrou (2017).
7 This section of the argument draws on Grahl and Lysandrou (2006), Lysandrou and Stoyanova (2007) and Lysandrou (2013a).
8 It was previously noted that Marx could not expand the commodity principle beyond its application to private human capacities and their material outputs given the circumstances of his time. As a result of this enforced limitation, he could not give a more than elementary account of the role of finance and of the financial markets in a commodity system, which in turn is why many heterodox economists and other social scientists look to Schumpeter or Keynes, and more latterly Minsky, rather than to Marx as guides to the financial world. However, the importance of Marx in understanding finance lies not so much in what he himself wrote on the subject as in his provision of the appropriate conceptual tools needed to achieve that understanding. Marx, we say, could not completely expand the commodity principle because of the economic and financial circumstances prevailing in his day; that expansion is only made possible from the viewpoint of contemporary economic and financial circumstances. Now, if we reverse the equation such that these contemporary circumstances are viewed from an expanded commodity standpoint, it becomes possible to gain an insight into these circumstances that is not otherwise possible. This is especially true of the ongoing expansion in size of the securities markets. One can make better sense of this development by approaching it from Marx's commodity angle rather than from the angle of more contemporary economists who, in the end, only see securities as financing instruments rather than as commodities in their own right and thus cannot provide a satisfactory framework for understanding finance's growing scale.

2 Genesis

2.1

The foregoing explanation of how a global commodity system has emerged gives rise to three questions: when, exactly, did the system emerge? Why did the system emerge when it did? And, finally, where is the system headed? These questions are answered in the order given.

2.2

A further major feature that distinguishes physical and commodity spaces concerns history. The history of human civilisation spans approximately 10,000 years, that is, from about 8000 BC to the present. This history, hugely complex and extremely rich in detail and colour, may not seem old when set against the history of the universe and that of our planet within it. By contrast, the history of physical space civilisation does seem old when compared with the history of the global commodity system simply because this system really has no history. Where the year AD 2000 marked yet another stage in the unfolding development of human civilisation, it on the contrary marked the very first stage of development of the global commodity system. As this system could not of course have emerged from nothing, it has to have had a prehistory, a history of coming into being as a more or less complete global commodity system. But even this prehistorical phase is a relative short one, spanning a mere 250 years from about 1750 to 2000.

To understand the importance of the year 2000, it first helps to work backwards from this date. The latter, it has been said, roughly marks the point at which the commodity principle has not only been stretched to cover virtually the entire surface of the planet but also deepened to cover the public capacity for activity in addition to the private capacities and to cover financial securities in addition to material outputs.

Now, if the eventual emergence of the global commodity system as a complete operational entity represents a certain critical phase of the commodity stretching-deepening dynamic, it must follow that the embryonic stage of development of that system must begin at that point in time when the stretching-deepening dynamic first comes into play. This is never the case before about 1750. Elements of the commodity exchange principle such as the use of money and the pricing and trading of goods against socially sanctioned standards appear in many early societies, but they do so only in a sporadic way with the result that this principle never gains sufficient weight of force as to displace the associative principle as the dominant organisational principle of society. This holds true to a large extent even in the post-medieval period spanning 1500 to 1750, one which sees a substantial growth in trade and commerce and a parallel growth of banks and the money markets. Although commodity relations in these centuries become a more established rather than transient feature in Western Europe, they still largely remain confined to a single category, that for goods and services, which is why the commodity exchange principle still remains subordinate to the associative principle.

The period around 1750 marks the tipping point in the development of a global commodity system, the point at which the commodity principle starts to come to the fore in a few localities, because this is when the principle is for the first time deepened to encompass the labour power and capital capacities. The major enabling factor behind this quantum leap in commodity development was the corresponding leap in scientific and technological development. Socially sanctioned production standards and prices can only become meaningful in the context of mass markets, and such markets can only emerge with the application of new scientific knowledge and new technological innovations in industry and in agriculture. The industrial and agricultural revolutions that began in earnest around 1750 facilitated not only an acceleration in the rate of supply of material produce but also an acceleration in the volume of demand for this produce by enabling the formation of a class of agents that, deprived of means of production, are forced to sell labour power for a money wage so as to access the markets for means of subsistence. As the capacity for labour becomes a commodity, so to that same degree does the capital capacity. The deployment of capital as a profit-generating capacity in various economic sectors may have increased in scope and intensity long before 1750, but it is only from about this point onwards that the capital capacity becomes a commodity subject to socially enforced pricing standards because it is only then that such standards become meaningfully operational, as explained earlier.

Relatively short as it is, the global commodity system's prehistory further divides into two sub-periods: that between 1750 and 1980 and that between 1980 and 2000. The first and much longer of these two sub-periods sees the gradual replication across different regions of the world of what are originally European commodity systems comprising the private capital and labour capacities on the one hand and material outputs on the other. This geographical stretching of the commodity principle had to overcome various sociopolitical impediments, chief of which were the colonial system that reached its global apogee by about 1900, and the communist system that grew to span about a third of the world's population after its first appearance in 1917 before eventually collapsing towards the end of the 20th century. Whatever the motivation behind colonial expansion, the fact is that this system rested on an organisational principle that was in direct contradiction to that which was central to the operation of the domestic political and economic systems of the European colonising countries. Where these countries combined physical space relations based on formal equality and freedom of choice with commodity space relations based on sales of capacities and outputs against socially established pricing standards, the colonial system which they operated rested solely on physical space relations based on inequality and the use of coercive force. With the dismantling of colonialism during the 20th century, a congruity of principles is established both in physical space as the former colonies become independent nation states, and in commodity space as commodity systems come into existence as genuinely recognisable systems in these newly independent states for the first time. As for the communist systems that flourished during the mid-part of the 20th century, no matter how advanced the institutional trappings and the technological resources at their disposal, their suppression of commodity exchange relations in favour of a near complete reliance on associative relations of central planning and state control meant that these systems essentially represented a throwback to a pre-commodity era.

The second, much shorter sub-period spanning 1980 to 2000 marks both a further continuity in commodity development and a further qualitative leap in that development. There is further continuity in that this period sees the near total collapse of communism and thus the consequent possibility for the geographical stretching of the commodity principle to reach a culminating, because genuinely global, stage of development. There is a further qualitative leap in that it is in this same short time span at the close of the 20th century that the commodity principle is now deepened to encompass government capacities in addition to the private capacities and financial securities in addition to material outputs. The reason for the commoditisation of the government capacity comes down to the increase in government dependence on the bond markets. From playing a minor role in domestic economies up to the 1930s, governments came to play a large and highly active role by 1980. However, what characterised this entire period is that governments were not usually both heavily and permanently dependent on bond issuance to fill the gaps in their financing needs. This is why they remained largely unencumbered by the market principle: they may have helped to ensure that private capacities for activity were deployed according to the rules of commodity exchange, but their own capacities for government remained outside of these rules. The situation changed after 1980 with the acceleration in the rate of government bond issuance (see Appendix A, Figure A.1) and with the corresponding growth in the financial pressures on governments. The reason why the commoditisation of financial securities after 1980 coincided with the commoditisation of government capacities comes down to the pricing of risk: corporate securities can only function as portable stores of value when the risks associated with their rates of return are factored into their prices, and government bonds can only effectively serve as the risk-free benchmarks against which corporate credit and equity risk premiums are calculated at the point when the large and permanent borrowing needs of governments ensure that there are ample supplies of their bonds across the maturity spectrum.

To say that the contemporary period marks the beginnings of a global commodity system as an operational totality is not to say that just about everything else about the contemporary world economy is also new. Rather, it is to distinguish what is new and original about that economy from what is old and traditional. If it was previously argued that physical space internationalisation and commodity space globalisation are the inverted opposites of each other, the argument here is that this opposition holds as much in a temporal sense as in a spatial one: where almost nothing about physical space internationalisation is new because almost nothing is without some historical precedent, almost everything about commodity space globalisation is new because almost everything here is without precedent. Let us again go back to the post-medieval period beginning around AD 1500. From a physical space perspective there may be some truth to the claim that this period marks the beginnings of a world system of international relations.[1] Yet it is also a period when there is not even the merest hint of a global commodity system given that the commodity principle continues to be confined to just one small fraction of just one entity type, material goods. Now let us scroll forward to the period around 1900. This marked a high point of physical space internationalism, characterised as it was by exceptionally large volumes of cross-border flows of people, goods and financial investments, all of which were in turn made possible by the revolutions in international transportation and communication systems. Yet it was also a period when there was still no global commodity system in any meaningful sense. International trade volumes may have been high, but, barring a few exceptions, these volumes did not result in any global harmonisation of production and pricing standards, which, on the contrary, largely remained localised. As for the financial realm in 1900, heavy international financial flows may have led to an international averaging out of required rates of return but not of risk-adjusted rates of return as risk in the international domain was something to be generally avoided.[2] Given that any accumulation of government debt was at that time typically treated as an unwelcome development, only to be allowed if and when special circumstances required it, government bonds did not serve as the risk-free benchmarks against which the risks on corporate securities could be calculated. Financial risks could be assessed and priced on an associative, face-to-face basis but not from a distance, and certainly not from an international distance. All of this is in contrast to today in that there is now a globally integrated system of risk benchmarks, at the core of which are the bonds of the governments of the world's most powerful economies, that allows for the pricing of financial risk from a distance. This point is absolutely crucial to the unprecedented scale of the contemporary financial system. It is because financial risk can now be priced against market standards rather than having to be privately assessed that securities have been transformed into stand-alone entities that can be traded away from their initial conditions of issuance,[3] and it is because of this transformation that the way is now open for the world's stocks of bonds and equities to grow to proportions that were previously unimaginable.

2.3

Turning to the question as to why the global commodity system emerge when it did, it must first be noted that physical and commodity spaces differ not only according to their age of development but also according to their mode of development. Human society in physical space does not evolve according to any single, determinate law of evolution. Rather, indeterminacy is the characterising feature here in that any uniformity of forward motion is typically overshadowed by a diversity of forms of that motion, in that any element of necessity or inevitability of outcome is just as inevitably shaped by the influence of chance and accident, and in that the constraints of structure can be, and often are, suppressed or distorted by the intervention of agency and volition. By contrast, commodity space does follow a single, determinate law of evolution. As long as the commodity principle is confined to a minority group of material goods or services, and thus kept on the exterior of society, as was the case right down to the 18th century, its further development can be blocked. However, once the commodity principle penetrates the interior of any one society and becomes its dominant organisational principle, its further advance to become the dominant principle of every other society in every other region of the planet is inevitable. That line of advance may come up against formidable barriers, it may be subject to breaks in continuity and it may even be temporarily thrown into reverse gear, but it will in the end always prevail and continue its forward trajectory and it will do so because of the superiority of the commodity principle over the only other major organisational principle that has ever existed until now, the associative principle. There can be no greater proof of that superiority than the failure and the collapse of the Soviet style communist experiment towards the end of the 20th century. That experiment can be said to have represented the final and severest stress test of the commodity principle on a global scale: final, because with the collapse of communism the associative principle has, at the most basic level of production at least, been relegated to a subordinate status in virtually every area of the planet; severest, because all of the resources and all of the 20th-century technologies available to the governments of the communist countries were deployed in the attempt to prove the superiority of central state planning over decentralised commodity exchange.

The source of the commodity principle's superiority can be traced to the interplay between technological progress and population growth in physical space. If, on the one hand, technological progress has the potential to generate an increase not only in the scale of production – the volume of material outputs that can meet population demand – but also in the complexity of production, the range and diversity of material outputs that can meet the manifold differences of population demand, on the other hand, it is the acceleration in population growth that, having been made possible by the opening up of these two potentialities, then requires their continuing and simultaneous fulfilment. A society based on the associative principle cannot accommodate this simultaneity: it can accommodate complexity but only by limiting activities to small communities of individuals, thus allowing production to meet particular needs; conversely, it can accommodate scale but only by suppressing complexity, because scale can only be achieved with the standardisation of production, and because standardisation in a society based on the associative principle presupposes the concentration of decision-making powers in the hands of a central organising authority, powers that in turn can only be effectively exercised by restricting the range of material outputs and by simplifying the rules of allocation and distribution. By contrast, a society in which the commodity principle encompasses both labour power and capital transcends the scale-complexity trade-off because of the dynamic interaction between these opposing commoditised capacities.

On the one side, the formation of a mass of wage-earning labourers necessarily forces production in the direction of standardisation: while some goods and services can still be made or provided to personal order and their prices negotiated on a face-to-face basis, in the more general case it is easier and cheaper for producers to put on offer a range of standardised products and invite customers to choose those products that suit their particular requirements. On the other side, the transformation of capital into a profit-earning capacity that is subject to the laws of commodity exchange necessarily forces constant change in production standards. Producers may introduce standards, but it is consumers, through the exercise of wage-backed demands, who have the ultimate power of sanctioning them. As owners of the capital capacity need to constrain wages to a market-set rate in order to generate profit, wage earners will generally look to those products that meet their requirements not only most adequately but also most cost-effectively. As technological progress constantly offers not only new ways of producing established goods but also opportunities of producing new types of goods that will be of use to consumers, it follows that a particular range of goods that are socially sanctioned at one point in time may be de-sanctioned at another point in time as wage earners switch to alternative goods that are considered superior in terms of quality or cost. It is the awareness of this possibility, combined with the profit incentive, which drives owners of capital to attempt to always be near, if not at, the forefront of innovation.

The interplay between technological progress and population growth that has driven the commoditisation of human capacities and of their material outputs is also ultimately that which has driven the commoditisation of financial securities. What has been central to this development is the radical change in the nature of government dependence on the bond markets that occurred towards the end of the

20th century. Where prior to this time governments would typically issue small amounts of securities or, if issuing large amounts, would only do so as a temporary measure to confront a particular emergency or to fund a particular project, their dependence on the bond markets has since then become both significant and permanent. The mounting pressures on domestic economies, not least of which are those stemming from rapid demographic change, require corresponding flows of government services to cope with those pressures. Faced with increasing demands on their capacity to govern, but at the same time faced with limits on the amounts of tax revenues that can be generated, governments have increasingly resorted to bond issuance as the means of bridging the gap. To have been able to do so, there needed to be on the demand side of the government bond markets an investor body large enough to accommodate the increased scale of government borrowing. The reality is that such a body does now exist courtesy of the very same demographic and other pressures that have forced governments into continually increasing their supply of bonds in the first place.

While other factors have played a role in the transformation of asset management into a mass industry, by far the most important is the move away from universal government provision of social and welfare services towards more selective forms of provision that give priority to the needs of the poorest and most vulnerable sections of the population. To cater for those mid- to high-income households who have been forced to make their own retirement and other welfare provisions, institutional investors have had to shift towards more standardised forms of asset management. While their very wealthy clients can still be personally advised as to how best to invest their money to attain certain investment targets, the more cost-effective approach for the less wealthy clients is to place on offer a wide selection of portfolios managed to specified combinations of risk and return and invite these clients to choose those portfolios whose advertised characteristics match their particular risk appetites. The commoditisation of securities links in as much with these structural changes in the asset management industry as with its growth in scale: given that the overall risk profile of an institutionally managed portfolio depends on the risk characteristics of its constituent securities, it follows that security issuing organisations need to be tied to strict transparency and behavioural constraints to safeguard not only the consistency with which their securities can serve as stores of value but also the consistency with which their securities can contribute to the overall risk-return profiles of the portfolios that are marketed to the public.

In helping to transform institutional asset management into a mass industry, governments have helped to create a large and stable demand not only for their own debt securities but also for those issued by banks and non-bank corporations. That the latter have been willing to take full advantage of the opportunities opened up by institutional investor demand for investable assets – despite the fact that this demand is contingent on compliance with strict transparency and governance standards – can be traced back to the same mix of pressures that have driven the increased issuance of government bonds. Take the case of banks that have traditionally relied primarily on household deposits to fund their loans to businesses and households. On the one hand, the fact that households are increasingly shifting their retirement savings out of bank deposits and into financial market investments in the search for yield explains why banks have had to increase their issuance of long-term bonds and short-term money market instruments to fill the gaps in the liability side of their balance sheets. On the other hand, the need to contain the pressures on the asset side of their balance sheets, while at the same time accommodating the ever-expanding demand for loans from businesses and households, explains why banks are increasingly bundling large parts of these loans into asset-backed securities that can then be sold to institutional asset managers and other large investors. Now take the large non-bank corporations that in an era of rapid technological change and thus ever-intensifying competition must have constant access to large external sources of funds to finance research and product development, to finance mergers and acquisitions, or to finance any of the other measures needed for survival. Business corporations have always tended to rely on a mix of debt and equity forms of external finance to supplement their funding needs in order to avoid an excessive concentration of risk on the one hand and an excessive dilution of the benefits of ownership and control on the other. What is now happening is that while the ratio of debt to equity forms of external funds raised by corporations remains fairly stable the ratio of bank borrowing to security market forms of funding is declining. The fact that bonds are tradable in a way that bank loans are not, and thus the fact that institutional investors do not need to be compensated for loss of liquidity in the way that banks must be when they extend loans, means that large corporations are increasingly relying on the bond markets for all but very short period borrowing requirements.

It is the pressures on governments and corporations to issue increasing amounts of securities to escape financing constraints, coupled with the pressures on institutional investors to buy increasing amounts of securities to meet their asset management needs, that have caused the global securities markets to grow to a size out of all proportion to the global real economy. While roughly equal in value to that for world annual output in 1980, the aggregate value of securities stocks was more than twice that of world annual output by the early 2000s (see Appendix A, Figure A.1). This growing disparity, which has been driven principally by the bond segment of the securities markets, inevitably begs the question as to just how far it can grow. The answer is that we simply do not know. We know that there must be limits to the amounts of debt securities that can be supported by the underlying real sector, but we just do not know what these limits are. Those who claim to know otherwise can only do so by invoking the lessons of history[4] but the fact of the matter is that history offers no lessons in this regard because something is happening today that is without historical precedent and that something is the colonisation of the future, its structuring and annexation as an auxiliary space of human habitation.[5] This development has not happened before because of the absence of the kind of the techniques required for the management and control of financial risk. Portfolio diversification is not new, but what is new is the scale of diversification as risk is spread not only within individual portfolios but also across portfolios, and not only across domestic portfolios but also across foreign portfolios. Derivatives are not new, but what is new is the scale of their use to strip out and sell on those risk components in securities that are not wanted while those components that are wanted are kept. Finally, and most importantly of all, what is new are not only the globally harmonised risk benchmarks already mentioned but also the type of transparency and governance constraints that are now imposed on governments and private corporations as a condition of financial market entry. These constraints are far tighter and far more comprehensive than anything seen in the past, and they are so principally because of the efforts on the part of institutional asset managers to safeguard the value storage function of financial securities. Ultimately, it is the institutional need to treat securities as value containers, to give them a quantitative dimension that they cannot have in the absence of governance standards and constraints, which holds the key to the spatialisation of the future. To use an analogy, just as the buildings, transportation systems, communications networks and so on constitute the necessary physical infrastructure that makes possible the production and trading of material outputs so do the new transparency requirements and governance rules and regulations constitute the infrastructure of time, the beams and pillars, the walls and floors that help to give body and shape to the future as an economic space fit for permanent occupation.

2.4

Just as the intervention of human agency and the roles of chance and accident have prevented any past possibility for events in physical space to unfold to any determinate pattern, so do these same factors prevent any possibility for predicting the precise form or manner in which events in this space will continue to unfold. Conversely, just as the inexorability with which local commodity systems have over the past two and half centuries expanded and coalesced to the point where a global commodity system is now an operational totality, so can it be reasonably predicted that this system will continue to mature and expand. This conclusion contrasts sharply with those drawn from an analytical framework that elevates the capital capacity to a position of primacy with the result that the global economic system is classified as a system of global 'capitalism'. To illustrate the point, consider two contrasting traditions within this alternative, and more conventional, framework, one which helped to inspire the construction of Soviet-style communism in the 20th century, and the other which was in its turn inspired by the collapse of communism at the end of that century.

To give analytical primacy to the private capital capacity and thus to classify the economic system based on commodity exchange as capitalism is to date the system from at least the mid-18th century. From this starting point it is then possible to divide capitalism's history into 'early', 'middle' and 'late' stages of development, from which position it is then but a short step to the conclusion that capitalism is ripe for overthrow and replacement by an alternative economic system. What drove the establishment of communism in the 20th century was not merely the belief that an economic system organised along the associative principle, in its central state planning form, was superior to a system organised along the commodity exchange principle but also the conviction that the centuries old system of capitalism was in a state of degeneration and decline, a conviction reinforced by the observed increase in the scale and amplitude of the recurrent crises afflicting the major market-based economies during the course of the 19th and 20th centuries. However, once the capital capacity is seen to be just one of the component parts of a complete commodity system that comprises the government capacity along with private capacities and that comprises financial securities along with material products, it then becomes possible to see that the 250-year period before the start of the 21st century was merely an incubatory period preparing the way for the birth of the global commodity system as an operational totality occupying its own global space. There will be a time when, having displaced the associative principle as the dominant organisational principle of society, the commodity exchange principle will itself be displaced in this role by another, even more superior, organisational principle. But that time is not now. The global dominance of the commodity principle may not last anything like as long as has the associative principle, but what is certain is that human civilisation has still some way to go before all the material and institutional prerequisites for a more advanced form of social organisation are in place.

The collapse of communism as a major alternative to commodity-based systems has given impetus to the idea that there are different forms or varieties of capitalism that can coexist in competition with each other for some time to come.[6] From the two-space perspective that has been deployed here, this idea can be seen to be wrong even while containing an element of truth. From a physical space standpoint, it is true that different countries and regions in the world can operate, and indeed must operate for reasons of social cohesion and stability, according to rules and regulations that, because of the continuing weight of historically conditioned customs and traditions, differ markedly from each other. From a commodity space standpoint, however, there is and there can only be one global commodity system comprising of individuals as possessors of capacities, of organisations as clusters of capacities and of countries as agglomerations of capacity clusters, all of which contribute to the production of a given stream of material commodities that can in turn support a given stock of financial commodities. In this commodity space, there are certainly differences between countries, but these differences are less a manifestation of different types of capitalism than of different levels of development and application of the commodity principle.

In the case of the communist systems created in the course of the last century, the suppression of the commodity principle was complete in the sense that it was not allowed to encompass any type of entity, whether goods and services, human capacities or financial securities. Today the suppression of the commodity principle is partial in that while in virtually every area of the world it is allowed to encompass goods and services, in many countries it is not allowed to encompass financial securities with the result that the private and public capacities for activity in these countries are only weakly exposed to the pressures of commodity exchange, namely those emanating from the product markets. In some cases, the domestic economies are simply too small to support securities markets of any significant size. However, in the many other cases where there is potential for security market expansion this potential remains largely unrealised. Part of the explanation for this state of affairs is that the policymakers in these countries continue to promote bank-based forms of finance because these relational forms fit more easily into plans for generating rapid economic growth and development. Another part of the explanation may be that the kind of transparency and governance standards that are required to develop deep and liquid securities markets are either politically inconvenient or orders of magnitude more difficult to establish and maintain than are the production standards for goods and services. But whatever the obstacles that have previously stood in the way of security market development and the consequent promotion of the commodity principle in finance in these economies, these obstacles will sooner or later have to be overcome for the same reasons as has happened in the advanced market economies of North America, Western Europe and certain other parts of the world.

Those reasons come down to the twin pressures of demographic and technological change. In those countries where the associative principle in finance continues to rule over the commodity principle, the entire financial burden incurred by their major organisations in the course of their operations must be borne by the associative relations linking these organisations both to each other and to the individuals that they serve. This situation may last in the short to medium term, but it is doubtful whether this can be the case in the longer term. Faced with ageing populations and a corresponding rise in dependency ratios, the governments in these countries will need to issue increasing amounts of long-term bonds to bridge the financing gaps that will likely widen in tandem with these developments. Similarly, faced with increasing gaps in the liability side of their balance sheets as households who live longer go elsewhere to earn better returns on their retirement savings, banks will have to issue increasing amounts of bonds to cover these gaps. Finally, corporations which need to be able to borrow large sums so as to finance any of the measures that are required to maintain a competitive position in the global product markets will increasingly switch from bank loans to bond issuance as a means of containing borrowing costs. In short, those countries with the potential to have large, deep and liquid securities markets must at some point or other realise that potential because as their economies grow and mature and as the financial burdens on their governments and private corporations grow accordingly, so will these organisations need to find ways of coping with these burdens and by far the most effective way is by dividing financial commitments into separate time compartments, some that can be dealt with in the present and the rest that can be dealt with at intermittent points in the future.

It is because every large economy must at some point colonise the future so as to make it take the overspill of the financial pressures of the present that explains why there cannot long continue to be different varieties of market-based systems in any meaningful sense. As already noted, different historically and culturally conditioned rules, customs and codes of conduct will persist in physical space, and, indeed, will be encouraged to persist, because these are necessary for ensuring the continuity of productive activity and output flow, which is in turn necessary to supporting a growing volume of financial securities. In commodity space, however, there has to be convergence towards globally harmonised transparency and governance standards, by which is meant convergence not only with respect to the behaviour of organisations taken in isolation but also with respect to their behaviour towards each other. The regulatory relations between governments and private corporations, the credit relations between banks and non-bank corporations, or the input-output relations between business corporations will at some point no longer be able to remain opaque and governed by privately ordered priorities and by privately negotiated terms of association. Rather, they will have to be opened up to scrutiny and made to conform with market-set standards of conduct because these are the preconditions imposed by the institutional asset management industry that is best positioned to absorb the volumes of securities on the scale required by issuers but which can only do so on the basis of the commoditisation of securities, their transformation into self-standing and portable value containers that can be passed from hand to hand and inserted into and extracted from portfolios at will.

2.5

To summarise, following a short, formative period that began around 1750, a global commodity system finally emerged as an operational totality by about 2000. The global ascendency of the commodity principle as the dominant organisational principle of society is due to its superior ability to accommodate the potentialities offered by technological progress in a way demanded by the pressures of population growth. There will continue to be scope for the further development and expansion of the global commodity system, particularly as regards countries' respective contributions to financial securities stocks. While the fact that these contributions remain at present highly uneven does not prevent the operation of the global commodity system, it does have a bearing on its mode of operation as will now be seen.

Notes

1 See e.g. the world systems theory of Wallerstein (1974).
2 To quote Stone writing about British overseas investments in the latter half of the 19th century: "The British financial press and investing public felt that high-yielding foreign bonds were synonymous with high risk. 5–6 per cent represented a fair return on a relatively risk-free investment: securities bearing a higher rate of return were to be avoided. The greatest part of debentures over the half-century, both government and joint-stock company obligations, fell safely within these limits" (Stone, 1999 p. 31).
3 The need to trade securities as stand-alone entities also explains the new rationale for corporate limited liability. See Lysandrou (2014a) for a discussion of this point.
4 A good example of this line reasoning is to be found in Reinhart and Rogoff (2009, 2010). For a rebuttal see Lysandrou (2013a).
5 See Lysandrou (2016) for a fuller account of this interpretation of financialisation (i.e. the growing weight of the world's securities markets relative to the world's product markets) as the colonisation of the future.
6 See e.g. Hall and Soskice (2001).

3 Operation

3.1

The global commodity system draws its operational dynamic from the interaction of two antithetical processes that are themselves in turn continually reinforced by that dynamic. These processes are described from the respective perspectives of individuals and countries before their interaction is examined more closely.

3.2

The line of development of human society in physical space may not be governed by any single law of evolution, but that line traces a forward-facing trajectory nonetheless. Physical space, in other words, is a space of human progression. The benefits of that progression that are palpable for the majority if not for the entirety of the world's population broadly fall into two categories: technological and political. Technological progression refers to the advances in human knowledge that translate into the creation of ever more advanced products and services that contribute in one way or other to the material well-being of individuals. Political progression refers to the diffusion of various rights and obligations that allow growing numbers of individuals to participate in some meaningful way in the running of their community, region or country.

Having emerged as an operational totality occupying its own socially constructed space, the global commodity system will continue to expand and mature, but as it does so, it will cause a continuing deterioration in the economic condition of the world's majority. Commodity space, in other words, is a space of regression. The root cause of this regression is exploitation, the appropriation by one group of individuals of a surplus produced by another group of individuals.[1]

Exploitation as so defined has taken place in physical space down the centuries, but what is now different is that, having largely disappeared from that space, the exploitation process has been transferred to commodity space. With this transfer of exploitation across spaces has come a corresponding transformation in its mode of operation. Exploitation in physical space was invariably based on the associative principle: whether the appropriation of a surplus took place within or across different geographical localities or regions, that appropriation was always and everywhere based on coercive relations involving groups of individuals who were in no doubt as to their position or place in those relations. By contrast, as a social construction that owes nothing to nature, and which exists solely through decentralised commodity exchanges, commodity space interposes itself between different groups of individuals in a way that keeps them separate and mutually indifferent to each other while at the same time providing the necessary intermediary medium that can facilitate exploitation.

That intermediary medium is the global expanse of values that has a fixed size at any fixed moment in time. Not all of the individuals who participate in the global economy are involved in the creation of the global material output made available at that moment. However, they are all involved in the creation of the corresponding global value expanse inasmuch as they all have sanctioning power over prices and thus the power of determining which particular material outputs conform to prevailing production standards and which do not and therefore which outputs are eligible for inclusion in the global value expanse and which are not. As the social determination of the values of material outputs also entails, on the one hand, the social determination of the values of the human capacities that are deployed in their production, and on the other hand, the social determination of the values of the financial securities that lay claim to future output streams, it follows that what individuals then subtract from the global value expanse essentially depends on the type and the volume of income-generating commodities that they each possess. Judged from the standpoint of these criteria, individuals broadly divide into three groups.

At one extreme and comprising the vast majority of those participating in the global commodity system are the individuals who possess a single income-generating commodity, their capacity for labour. While the wage share of total global income is proportionately significant, that share in no way corresponds to the proportionate numbers of wage earners. On the contrary, far from increasing in line with the continuing increase in these numbers, the wage share of aggregate global income is in fact declining.[2] The principal sources of the downward pressure on wages have been the rapid advances in transportation and communication technologies inasmuch as they induce ever-increasing wage competition, not only because they reduce the numbers of available jobs as a consequence of mechanisation, but also because they make possible, or hold up the threat of making possible, the transfer of jobs from one wage earning area to another, lower wage earning area. The collapse of communism towards the end of the last century was a particularly significant contributory event in this regard, for where that collapse served to release huge reservoirs of labour onto the global labour pool, the ongoing technological advances ensured that much of that pool was harnessed to the operation of the global commodity system, a further drag on global wage growth being an inevitable concomitant. Finally, in addition to the expansion and closer integration of the global labour markets, a further source of the downward pressure on the wage share of global income has been the expansion of the global securities markets. This is because if the institutional and other investors on the demand side of these markets need to have guarantees as to the rates at which monies are returned to them, those managing the corporations and governments on the supply side can only be in a position to give such guarantees, while at the same time safeguarding their own income rewards, by keeping wage increases as low as possible.

Where at one extreme, the majority of those participating in the global commodity system collectively put far more into the global space of values than they take out, at the other extreme there is a tiny minority of participants that take out far more from that space than they put in. These are the high net worth individuals (HNWIs), to use the now common classification of those people whose assets excluding their primary residence exceed $1 million. In addition to holding wealth in other forms such as cash and investments of passion (works of art, etc.), the bulk of their wealth is stored in income-generating assets that include alternative investments (investments in hedge funds and private equity firms), real estate and, above all, equity and debt securities. Institutional asset managers may be the principal investors pushing for the commoditisation of securities so as to safeguard their value storage property, but it is wealthy individuals who are among the major beneficiaries of this commoditisation, as attested by the fact that currently over one half of global HNWI wealth is held in the form of financial securities.[3] There are various routes through which vast sums of income-generating wealth come to be concentrated in the hands of a few HNWIs, but the following appear to be the most common. The first is the now entrenched tendency to reward the top executives of banks and non-bank corporations with equity-linked bonuses that are often many multiple times the value of their annual salaries. A second route is through family inheritance of a significantly sized amount of wealth that, absent bad management, can beget more wealth simply through reinvestments in the original family business, through diversifying into other business ventures or through a mix of both strategies. A third route is through technological invention and product innovation: not all new inventions or new products will be socially sanctioned, but those that are can generate huge rewards for their inventors or originators given the global scale of market demand, rewards that, once again, can beget even more rewards through diversification into other income-generating assets. Finally, a fourth major route through which personal wealth can be amassed pertains to the way that certain individuals who have or develop a distinctive skill, talent or character trait that separates them from other individuals in their particular field or medium, such as sport or entertainment, use that distinctiveness to generate rewards above the average for their peers. The absolute size of these rewards can vary with the breadth of reach of the field or medium in question, but in an age when rapid technological advance has greatly expanded the geographical reach in many cases, the potential for generating rich rewards that can then be diversified into other income-generating assets has risen considerably.

The middle group of participants in the global commodity system, a group that is at once significantly larger than the super-rich at one end of the system and significantly smaller than the relatively poorer individuals at the other end, are those who in physical space run their own small businesses, occupy mid-managerial positions in corporate or government organisations or have highly skilled professions. In addition to being in possession of a capital, government or skilled labour capacity, some will also possess real estate over and above their primary residence and some will have investments in financial securities either directly or through professional intermediaries. The upshot of this observation is that the respective amounts of value that this middle group of individuals extract from the aggregate value expanse are far more variegated than is the case for the other two groups, with some at the lower end only extracting slightly more than is the average for those whose sole income-generating commodity is their labour power, others at the upper end extracting so much more as to be close to, if not actually part of, the HNWI category, and the rest spread across the entire income and wealth spectrum with their exact position being determined by the types and by the volumes of commodities in their possession.

The boundaries dividing the three groups of individuals listed earlier will change continually over time, but what is just as certain is that they will do so in accordance with a continuing acceleration of surplus appropriation and a continuing concentration of ownership of that surplus because of the continuing operation of two growth rate asymmetries in global commodity space: the horizontal asymmetry between the growth rate of labour power supply and that of the supply of the capital capacity and the vertical asymmetry between the growth rate of financial securities stocks and that of material output. As noted, the contradiction in the increasing abundance of labour power made possible by the combination of technological progress, political change and population growth is that this abundance results in an ever-expanding global value expanse while also ensuring an ever-contracting wage income share of that expanse. Add to all this the increased threats of job loss or job transfer made possible by technological progress and the result is not only a contraction in the aggregate share of wage income but also an increasing dispersion of income levels within that aggregate share as the rates of wage increase for different groups of wage earners vary according to their degree of exposure to the aforementioned threats. As for the growing weight of financial securities stocks relative to the material output streams to which they lay claim, this development helps not only to further depress the wage income share of the value expanse in favour of the profit share, but also to constrain those parts of this profit share accruing to the capital and government capacities deployed in the production of output, thus creating more room for the income shares received by the holders of securities. In effect, the continuing growth of securities stocks relative to the material output base is contributing not only to the continuing dispersion of income levels and wealth holdings across the income and wealth spectrum, but also to the continuing concentration of wealth holdings at the very top end of the spectrum as those individuals who come, through one route or other, to control a financial portfolio of a critical size are then able to generate a higher than average rate of wealth accumulation as returns are reinvested in more financial assets to generate more returns and so on in an accelerating upward spiral.

3.3

The antithetical processes of progression and regression are as evident at the level of countries as they are at that of individuals. Progression in physical space, it has been said, broadly comprises two dimensions: technological, the advance of scientific and technological knowledge, and political, the proliferation of the rules and rights of democracy and formal equality. Following the collapse of colonialism and communism over the course of the last century, progression in the latter, political sense has been experienced doubly by the peoples of countries previously subjected to external controlling pressures in that their acquisition of democratic rights at the individual level has been accompanied by the acquisition of the rights of sovereign independence at the national level. At the same time, the regression in commodity space that is experienced by the majority of the world's population is doubly experienced by most of those people living in countries that are on the periphery of the global commodity system in that this peripheral position generally leads these counties to make a greater net positive contribution to the global value expanse than would otherwise be the case.

While many of the countries currently on the periphery of the global commodity system have been former colonies, there are others that have never undergone this experience and, indeed, there are even some that were themselves former oppressors of other countries. The explanation for this disparity between physical space core-periphery relations in previous historical eras and commodity space core-periphery relations in the contemporary era comes down to the difference in the criteria by which such relations are established and maintained. As concerns physical space, there were in the past a variety of ways in which one country's control over another could be exercised while keeping to the common principle of direct association. This variety was exemplified by the fact that country size was not always a key determinant of direct control. Russia may have relied on its vast geographical size in exercising its authority and domination over its territorial neighbours down the centuries, but Britain and other West European countries, by virtue of their technological and military superiority, among other factors, were able to control international empires that comprised geographical areas many times the size of their own and that contained populations many times larger than their own. By contrast, country size in global commodity space is the only factor determining the positions respectively occupied by different countries in that space.

Recall that countries in commodity space are agglomerations of capacities and clusters of capacities, which means that their sizes relative to each other are here measured either according to the aggregate value of annual output flows generated by their capacities or according to the aggregate value of the outstanding stocks of debt and equity securities that are supported by their capacities. While the size asymmetries separating countries in material commodity terms often bear no direct resemblance to their size asymmetries in physical space as determined by land mass and population numbers, the asymmetries separating countries in financial commodity terms are far greater still. Thus, the USA with barely 5% of the world's population currently accounts for over 40% of the world's securities stocks while at the other end of the spectrum there are several emerging market economies with large populations that account for very small percentage amounts of the world's securities stocks (see Appendix A, Table A.1 and Figure A.2). These disparities come down to the wide divergences in the extent to which a production base on a sufficient scale and a governance infrastructure of a sufficient strength are combined together such as can allow for the creation and maintenance of substantial securities stocks. Thus, some countries may have a large domestic production base but weak governance institutions, and other countries may have strong governance institutions but a relatively small production base, while the US by contrast is unique in that it is at present the only country in the world that meets both the production size criterion and the governance strength criterion (only by joining their countries together in a currency union does the Eurozone group come close to matching the US on these criteria). At a time when securities stocks are increasingly dominating the underlying material output base on which they rest, it is the dominant contribution to these stocks made by the US that explains why that country sits at the very core of the global commodity system able to control and exploit countries on its periphery through the gravitational pull of mass rather than through the use of coercive force.

The cardinal issue in this regard is the US dollar's hegemonic position in the international currency system. In physical space, this hegemony makes little sense given that the persistent US trade and government deficits would seem to make it difficult for that country to service its large volumes of outstanding debt securities.[4] However, dollar hegemony makes every sense in commodity space in that US bonds here appear not only as types of debt but also as types of value containers that combine together with US equities to give the dollar a huge backing mass of such containers. It is this backing mass that explains why the dollar is the currency of choice for a multiple set of uses in an international context, including as an international medium of exchange, as a reserve currency and as an exchange rate anchor for other currencies. And it is this same backing mass that enables the US to control other countries from afar inasmuch as it enables its central authorities to conduct their domestic economic policies without reference to the actions of any other central authority while the converse is not generally true. The crux of the matter is that the sheer size and depth of the US financial markets enable them to provide strong protective cover against the effects of any sharp change in the dollar's exchange rate against other currencies: any such change will have differential effects on different parts of the US economy that may then cause upstairs portfolio shifts in the US financial markets, but as these shifts occur within the same dollar-denominated mass of financial securities, they do not further aggravate the change in the dollar's exchange rate, thus preventing any further amplifying effects on the underlying real economy. In sum, it is because the mass of financial securities behind the US dollar acts as a kind of currency shock absorber that explains why US policymakers can treat the dollar's international exchange rate with benign neglect when formulating policy. By contrast, in the case of countries with small domestic security markets, any portfolio investment shifts across securities triggered by the domestic economic impact of any sharp exchange rate change will likely also take the form of cross-currency shifts that may in turn amplify the initial exchange rate change and hence its impact on the underlying real economy. In short, the very smallness of the security markets of these countries can cause these markets to act as currency shock amplifiers, which is why the governments of these countries must make currency stability one of their major policy priorities and thus why, in order to keep to this particular priority, so many of them tie their currency's exchange rate to the US dollar regardless of any loss of policy autonomy entailed by this course of action.

The reason why the dollar financial markets allow not only for the exercise of US control from a distance but also for the extraction of a surplus by the US from countries with much smaller financial markets comes down to the substantial quantitative differences in the risk premiums that are factored into the prices of securities. If the large size of the US domestic economy and the fairly uniform application of transparency and governance standards across the US corporate and government sectors contribute to the depth of the US bond and equity markets, these factors taken in conjunction also explain why US securities typically carry lower than world average risk premiums. These include lower liquidity risk premiums (due to the depth of the US securities markets and hence the ease of trading with minimal price impact); lower sovereign risk premiums (due to the scale of US domestic economic activity and hence the corresponding scale of government taxation power); lower credit risk premiums (due to the higher level of trust in US corporate adherence to governance standards in addition to their adherence to production standards); and lower currency risk premiums (due to the range of choice of US asset classes across which investment funds can be moved according to exchange rate fluctuations or according to any other change in the economic environment). Thus, the end result of the size asymmetries separating the US securities markets at one extreme from the securities markets of most other countries at the other extreme is that while foreign investors tend to invest trillions of dollars more in US securities than do US investors in foreign securities they at the same time tend to earn billions of dollars less from their US holdings than do US investors from their foreign holdings.[5]

All countries with small securities markets are currently net losers regardless of the size of their real economies and the strength of their trading position. In other words, even countries with balance of trade surpluses are not able to offset the net losses incurred by the relative underdevelopment of their domestic securities markets. The case of China exemplifies the point. To maintain its high rate of job expansion, China continues to pursue an export-led growth strategy, the success of which depends on keeping its currency's exchange rate against the US dollar within a target range so as to maintain international price competiveness. To keep to this target range, China has to hold substantial reserves of US Treasuries on which the yield is typically negligible. In effect, China and several other emerging market economies in a similar position are caught in a new form of unequal exchange with the US inasmuch as the adverse terms of trade that they face arises not from the exchange of material commodities for other material commodities so much as from the exchange of material commodities for financial commodities. Of course, certain large institutions and wealthy individuals based in these emerging economies can seek to increase the foreign yields that they earn by diversifying away from US Treasuries and investing in the US corporate bond and equity markets, but to the extent that their investments reinforce the size of the dollar securities markets and hence the US' position at the core of the global commodity system, so too do they reinforce the peripheral position of their own countries.

3.4

This discussion points to a further reason why the start of the 21st century represents a critical juncture in the history of human development. It is that for the first time in that history the majority of the world's societies now operate to the same, globally uniform, law of motion: circular motion. Prior to 1750, no single law of societal development was possible because the continuing domination of the associative principle precluded the emergence of a parallel social space alongside physical space, thus allowing the different societies occupying this latter space to operate according to their own specific rules and customs and to develop according to their own particular growth trajectory. The interaction between societies that were in relatively close physical proximity to each other within Europe, Asia and other continents in the world may have led to certain converges in social practices and to certain similarities in the pace and mode of development, but these convergences and similarities largely remained bounded within the different continents. This state of affairs continued to hold for much of the time between 1750 and 2000 in that while this period saw the gradual ascendency of the commodity principle to become the dominant societal principle, it was only towards the end of the 20th century that the commodity principle's ascendency reached the point of enabling the completion of a global social space that parallels world physical space and thus of ensuring that the majority of the world's societies now become subject to the constraints of this social space. For this majority, and from this time onwards, entrapment in circular motion is their common fate as the positive force of progression in physical space and the negative force of regression in commodity space continually interact in a mutually reinforcing and mutually offsetting dynamic. The fact that some few individuals and some few countries can escape proregression, as the conjunction of progression and regression can be called, may give hope that this possibility of escape is open to all other individuals and to all other countries. However, this hope is illusory for in the absence of any consciously coordinated control of the newly emergent global commodity system it will operate in a way that promotes continual technological, institutional and other advances in physical space only so as to promote continual exploitation and marginalisation in commodity space.

Let us again go back to the case of individuals whose sole income-generating commodity is their labour power. On the one side, the material and social advantages offered by technological and political progress in physical space serve to promote these individuals' ambitions for personal advancement and their aspirations for a quality of life superior to that which was possible for previous generations. On the other side, however, the fact that the vast majority of the goods and services needed to sustain modern living have been commoditised means that any real scope for individual workers to have freedom of mobility and the means of realising their ambitions and aspirations requires that the price of labour power keeps pace, at the very least, with the prices of other commodities. This is simply not happening. Instead, the rate of wage increases is on average lagging behind the rate of increase of other commodity prices due to the downward pressure on wages exerted by an ever-expanding global labour pool. The result is a perpetual tightening of the constraints on working people's freedom of movement, action and choice. In effect, the constraints that used to be located in physical space, but have now been largely eliminated there due to the dissolution of personal ties of association and dependence, have been relocated in commodity space. Proregression and an ensuing entrapment in circular motion stem from this constant interaction between freedom and constraint, between the aspirations for a better quality of life that are continually reinforced by the manifold forms of physical space progression and the impediments blocking the realisation of these aspirations that are continually reinforced by the widening gap between average wage incomes and average living costs. Debt may offer a temporary escape from this circularity, but for the majority of those taking out debt in one form or other, this course of action over the longer run can only lead to a further tightening of the constraints on individuals' aspirations and freedom of movements, as interest payments have to be serviced in addition to meeting other living costs.

The fact that a few countries continue to dominate the world's financial securities stocks even while these stocks are increasingly dominating the world's material output base explains the widening gaps between countries as much as the widening gaps between individuals. The point is that countries that have achieved political independence can only achieve material progression through integration into the world economy, an integration which means bringing the national currency into relation with every other national currency belonging to every other country similarly integrated into the world economy. However, in a global commodity space overwhelmingly dominated by the securities markets of a few countries, the relations between the national currencies of countries with small securities markets cannot be established directly but indirectly via their common relation to the dominant national or regional currencies into whose orbits they have been drawn by the gravitational pull of these currencies. Given the disproportionate distribution of the costs and benefits in the contemporary currency hierarchy described earlier, it follows that for most of the countries on the periphery of the currency system the gains of continuing forward progression in physical space due to trade, investment and other forms of economic integration are continually counteracted by the losses of regression in commodity space caused in one way or other by currency colonisation.

While the absence of any coordinated control of the global commodity system means that its operation continually reinforces regression, that regression in turn continually reinforces the need for political control in physical space. From a two-space perspective, globalisation is conditional on localisation because, as was argued earlier, the continuity of material output flow needed to support an increasing volume of financial securities in commodity space is conditional on social and political stability in the physical localities where the producing organisations are based. The further argument here is that as the increasing pace of regression in global commodity space is bound to exacerbate social divisions and tensions at the country or regional level, it follows that there must be a corresponding strengthening of state power and control as a means of containing those divisions and tensions. At the inter-country level, the whole dual process is magnified, first, in the sense that the relocation of core-periphery relations between countries away from physical space and into commodity space leads to a magnification of regression for the majority of the peoples occupying countries in a peripheral position, and, second, in the sense that this magnification of regression can potentially heighten cross-border instability through population movements as much as intra-border instability. In this context, the decolonisation process in physical space and the achievement of national independence have as much to do with the exigencies of maintaining domestic order and of securing external borders as with the reclamation and assertion of national identity.

In the end, the fact that economic regression for the majority of the world's population is as much a key outcome of the dynamics of the global commodity system as technological and political progression means that the system is prone to the same fundamental contradiction that has afflicted every previous locally or regionally established commodity system: namely, that the contradiction which helps to give propulsion is also that which can cause disruption and breakdown. Although a commodity system is sustained not by central control but by the decentralised commodity exchange actions of all participating individuals, it can continue to function normally and in a self-sustaining way as long as there is universal adherence to the two cardinal rules of commodity exchange: the quantitative rule, i.e. that in any market the volume of entities put on offer does not deviate significantly for any significant length of time from the volume of demand, and the qualitative rule, i.e. that in every market there is a standard of production or a standard of provision against which the entities put on offer can be compared and priced accordingly. It is when the process of regression that is inherent in any commodity system intensifies to the point where it causes these rules to be breached that the system breaks down. Given the heightened scale and pace of regression presaged by the emergence of a global commodity system at the end of the 20th century, it was inevitable that it would not be long into the 21st century before the internal rules of the system would be breached.

3.5

To summarise, the contradiction inherent in the commodity principle is that it can promote social progress at rates that are not possible on the basis of the associative principle while at the same time facilitating exploitation and inequality on scales that are far greater than anything made possible by the associative principle. With the stretching and deepening of the commodity principle to the point where a global commodity space has emerged as a space in its own right distinct from, while also interdependent with, world physical space, that contradiction has also accordingly assumed global proportions. In facilitating world physical space progression on all fronts, technological and political, and on all levels, that of individuals and countries, the global proliferation of the commodity principle thereby results in a similar scale of regression in global commodity space. At the present time, the majority of the world's individuals who possess only their labour power as their income-generating commodity and the majority of the world's countries situated on the periphery of that space are subtracting a percentage share of the global expanse of values that is declining in inverse proportion to their percentage share of numbers. Conversely, the minority of the world's individuals who possess different and multiple types of income-generating commodities and the minority of the world's countries that are situated at the core of global commodity space are subtracting a percentage share of the global value expanse that is increasing in inverse proportion to their percentage share of numbers. The regression that is an integral part of the dynamics of the global commodity system need not cause that system to go into crisis and breakdown as long as the rate of regression is kept within certain bounds such that the system is not forced to breach its internally set limits. However, if the rate of regression does reach a point that leads to those limits being breached, then at that point there is a possibility that the system will go into a crisis. That possibility became reality with the global financial crisis of 2007–8.

Notes

1 The theory of exploitation expounded here was first developed in Lysandrou (1996, 2000, 2011a).
2 See e.g. the recent data supplied in Karabarbounis and Neiman (2013).
3 See e.g. Goda and Lysandrou (2014).
4 See Karltenbrunner and Lysandrou (2017) for a critique of those authors who are sceptical of continuing dollar hegemony in the face of continuing US trade and government deficits.
5 See e.g. the data for the early 2000s supplied by Forbes (2010).

4 Crisis

4.1

The financial crisis of 2007–8 was the first crisis of the global commodity system and therefore was the first crisis of its kind.[1] To say this is not to deny that there have been previous economic crises whose scale and reach of consequence were at least as significant as those of the 2007–8 crisis. The economic crisis following the Wall Street crash of 1929 is a case in point. The difference, rather, lies in the locus of crisis origin. In all previous crises that locus was invariably to be found in a particular national domain, even when, as in the 1929 case, there may have been serious international repercussions. What singles out the 2007–8 financial crisis is that its root causes were global in content, even though it first exploded in a tiny corner of the US financial sector. Indeed, it is precisely because of all of the pressures arising out of all of the regressive processes inherent in the newly operational global commodity system had come to be concentrated on a small number of financial instruments created by a small number of financial institutions over a small span of time that explains why the explosive force of the 2007–8 crisis was so immensely powerful.

4.2

The financial products at the epicentre of the financial crisis of 2007–8 were a specific type of debt security, collateralised debt obligations (CDOs). The best way to understand these securities and their relation to the other, more conventional, type of debt securities is to look at the 'floor', so to speak, where the ultimate source of the interest payments is to be found. Thus, the bonds issued by governments and corporations can be classified as 'ground floor' securities in that the cash flows on these securities are serviced directly out of tax revenues or corporate profits. The asset-backed securities (ABSs) issued by banks are 'first floor' securities in that the cash flows on them are serviced by the interest payments on various types of bank loans to customers, the most typical in terms of volume being residential mortgage loans. CDOs are essentially 'second floor' securities, structured financial products created by pooling nonconforming mortgage-backed securities, that is, securities backed by subprime and other types of nonconforming loans, together with conforming mortgage-backed securities as collateral for CDOs. Although it was well known that nonconforming loans taken on their own could in no way serve as safe collateral, it was believed that this problem could be circumvented by first mixing these loan-backed securities together with conforming loan-backed securities as collateral and then by using various techniques to enhance the creditworthiness of the structured securities, the three principal techniques being over-collateralisation (the volume of backing assets held is greater than the volume of securities issued), subordination (interest payments on super senior and senior securities are made first, and only then are holders of the mezzanine tranche securities paid, and so on, in descending order) and insurance (the senior tranches are given insurance cover by a sponsoring bank, an insurance company or monoline insurer). The problem was that the same credit enhancement techniques (CETs) that were intended to make CDOs safe also made them so complex and opaque as to break the central rule of commodity exchange.

Recall that for the price of any commodity to be set to a market standard, the characteristics of the commodity have to be sufficiently transparent as to allow for a broad customer base. Government and corporate debt securities generally meet this criterion, and so do ABSs inasmuch as their backing collateral consists of a single, homogenous class of assets (mortgage loans, car loans, credit card loans etc.). By contrast, the CDOs that were created in the run-up to the financial crisis did not meet this transparency criterion. Given that the securities that backed CDOs consisted of many different types of asset classes, and given the many different ways that these assets could be mixed together, it followed that no two CDOs were alike: each was a unique, customised product that could be sold at a privately negotiated price, but not so easily marketed on any standardised pricing terms. Thus, when the delinquency rate among US sub-prime borrowers began to rise sharply in the wake of the increases in the federal funds rate from mid-2004, not only did these sophisticated techniques not prevent a resulting fall in the prices of CDOs, they actually helped to accelerate the rate of that fall by virtue of having helped to make these products too opaque and hence too difficult to value accurately. It was the panic caused by the unexpectedly rapid collapse of the CDO market that led to the breakdown in trust between the large commercial banks, a breakdown that proved to be catastrophic in that it was the catalyst setting in motion a liquidity-solvency crisis spiral that eventually culminated in the paralysis of the whole financial system.

In addition to the opaque quality of CDOs, it was the quantity of these products that was key to triggering the financial crisis. In 2002, the total volume of CDOs outstanding came to about $250 billion. Had the market for CDOs remained that small in 2007, it is doubtful whether its collapse in the summer of that year would have had much of an impact. The fact of the matter, however, is that it had by then grown twelvefold to about $3 trillion, in other words, to a size sufficient to precipitate the financial crisis. There is no question that various failures within the financial system itself were instrumental to the rapid growth of these toxic securities, failures that included: the quest for fees and commissions on the part of the mortgage brokers and banks originating the sub-prime loans; the highly leveraged and chronically under-capitalised positions of the banks and of their investment vehicles; flaws in the risk assessment methods used by the credit-rating agencies to rate the various financial products created by the investment banks; and last but by no means least, the lack of proper oversight of the whole banking system on the part of the regulatory authorities. Important as were these institutional and regulatory failures to the growth of CDOs, however, they were so only in an enabling role, not in a causal one. Had they had causal primacy, one would have expected to see the growth of these securities in particular, and of ABSs more generally, develop over a much larger time span than was actually the case. ABSs had been introduced in the US in the early 1970s, and yet of the $9 trillion US ABS stocks outstanding in mid-2007, well over a half had been created in the preceding four years (see Appendix B, Figure B.1). Similarly, CDOs had been introduced in the US as early as the 1980s and yet the market for these products remained fairly small right up to the end of 2002, after which point it then suddenly exploded in size (see Appendix B, Figure B.2). The rapid acceleration in the supplies of ABSs and CDOs in such a short time span gives strong indication that causal primacy in the growth of these markets lay with demand pull pressures emanating from US and foreign investors' need for extra quantities of yield bearing securities.

The new millennium marked not only the point when a global commodity system became operational but also the point when the global demand for financial securities in their capacity as stores of value began to outstrip the global supply of these securities. Given the preponderant weight of the US securities markets in the global financial system, and the corresponding international status of the US dollar as the major reserve currency, it was inevitable that the global excess demand for securities would manifest in the US markets. While a significant part of foreign investment inflows into the US continued to be channelled into the US equity markets up to about mid-2001, the vast majority of these inflows were subsequently redirected into the US bond markets following the end of the dot-com bubble (see Appendix B, Figure B.3). The huge increase in foreign public and foreign private demand for US Treasury, municipal and corporate bonds, coupled with a continuing increase in domestic US private investor demand for these same securities, led to a continuing fall in their yields (see Appendix B, Figure B.4). It was chiefly in order to meet the excess investor demand for yield-bearing securities that the US banking sector started to accelerate the rate of supply of ABSs from about 2003. Despite this acceleration, however, the pressure of aggregate foreign and domestic demand in the US ABS market continued to be so strong and the consequent ABS spread over treasuries so low that the US asset shortage problem continued to be an acute one. This is where the CDOs enter the picture, for there can be no other plausible explanation for the sudden explosion in the rate of supply of these high-risk but high-yielding products from 2003 onwards than that it was chiefly motivated by the pressure of investor demand for yield spilling over from the other US bond markets. Indeed, this pressure was so great that the pace of production of cash CDOs simply could not keep up with the pace of demand, with the result that synthetic CDOs – i.e. artificial CDOs created by taking cash CDOs as their underlying reference entities in credit default swap arrangements between counterparties – increasingly became the dominant component of total CDO supply (as can be seen in Appendix B, Figure B.2). Of the $3 trillion worth of CDOs outstanding in mid-2007, approximately two thirds of this total were synthetic CDOs, products that had barely existed in 2002.

Given the strength of investor demand for CDOs emanating from outside of the banking sector, the question arises as to why a substantial proportion of these securities continued to be held within that sector. At the time of the sub-prime crisis of mid-2007, hedge funds held about 47% of all CDOs, other non-bank financial institutions such as pension funds and insurance companies held about 28%, while US and European banks held the remaining 25%. Although this figure represented only a quarter of all CDOs held, it was still a sum significant enough to have caused a widespread collapse in trust in the US and

European banking sectors when the toxic nature of CDOs became apparent. The answer to the question would at first seem to be that the banks were simply maximising profits by exploiting the interest differential between the rates on CDOs and on other long-term assets on the one hand and short-term borrowing rates on the other. In other words, it would seem that the banks' heavy involvement on the demand side of the CDO market constituted an arbitrage story quite separate from the story concerning non-bank investors' search for yield. However, close scrutiny of the events just prior to the financial crisis shows that the heavy bank involvement on the demand side of the CDO market was exactly part of the same investor search for yield story. In the run-up to the crisis, the banks were not issuing short-term commercial paper in order to buy CDOs. Rather, it was by then the other round: they were buying CDOs to use as collateral in the production of the commercial paper demanded by institutional investors.

4.3

At the time of the financial crisis, the three principal financial vehicles at the centre of the securitisation process were the special purpose entities (SPEs) that used mortgage and other credit loans as collateral for ABSs, the structured investment vehicles (SIVs) that used the securities issued by SPEs as collateral in the creation of CDOs and the conduits that, in contrast to the other two types of securitisation vehicles, specialised in the creation of short-term securities, asset-backed commercial paper (ABCP). While some conduits used an assortment of credit loans as backing collateral (single-seller and multi-seller conduits), others used an assortment of structured securities such as ABSs and CDOs (securities arbitrage and SIV conduits) while yet others used a combination of loans and structured securities (hybrid conduits). By mid-2007, the US ABCP market was by far the world's largest, accounting for $1.2 trillion of the then world total market size of $1.5 trillion, with bank-owned or bank-sponsored conduits accounting for the bulk of the US market, $900 billion of the $1.2 trillion.[2]

A fact that is just as striking as the commanding size of the US ABCP market in 2007 was the exceptionally short time span over which this size was reached. Although first established in the 1980s, the rate of growth of this market remained fairly moderate right up to the end of 2004 when that rate then suddenly exploded with the result that in the next two and a half years to mid-2007, the market had roughly doubled in size, from just over $600 billion to $1.2 trillion (see Appendix B, Figure B.5). The catalyst behind the huge acceleration in the rate of

US ABCP supply was the huge rise in institutional investor demand for this paper. Prior to 2004, the banks may still have been motivated to exploit the profit opportunities of borrowing short term to lend long term, but if this profit motive did not translate into the same high rate of ABCP supply as was seen after 2004, it was simply because there was at that time not enough investor demand for ABCP. It was only from the end of 2004 that this demand began to gather pace, and the principal reason for this was the continuing rise in the federal funds rate to which the rate on ABCP was closely linked right up to August 2007.

Recall that the early 2000s saw a steep rise in US mortgage lending as US banks sought to create the basic raw material needed for ABSs and cash CDOs, a rise that was to some degree facilitated by the easing of US monetary policy following the end of the dot-com boom. From 6.5% in late 2000, the federal funds rate fell to 1% in June 2003 where it remained until June 2004. However, just as the low short-term interest rate period gave boost to mortgage lending, that boost in turn helped to usher in a period of high short-term interests when the Federal Reserve, concerned about the possible inflationary consequences of increased consumer spending fuelled in part by the wealth effects of rising house prices, raised the federal funds rate by a quarter percent at a time in 17 consecutive steps starting in June 2004. In preceding periods of monetary policy tightening, the yield on 10-year Treasuries kept track with the target federal funds rate. On this occasion, however, it did not. While the policy rate fell by 5.5% between 2001and 2004, the yield on 10-year Treasuries fell by only 3.57%, from 6.77% to 3.2%; even more unusual, however, was that while the policy rate rose by 4.25% to 5.25% between mid-2004 and mid-2007, the yield on 10-year Treasuries rose by only 2% over the same period, to 5.2%, a development that has come to be described as the bond yield conundrum (see Appendix B, Figure B.6). Conundrum or not, the fact that the short-term rate remained above the long-term rate for much of the 2005–7 period made it inevitable that institutional investors would look to the short-term securities market as a supplementary means of satisfying their need for yield. The strongest indication that this was the case was the pattern of demand for US ABCP emanating from the US money market mutual funds (MMMFs).

MMMFs first emerged in the US in the early 1970s to exploit the opportunity offered by the regulatory cap on the interest that banks could pay on deposits. As the cap was set at a rate below money market yields, the MMMFs provided households with a profitable alternative to bank deposits in that while offering the same level of safety (MMMFs invest only in such short-term assets as to be able to maintain a stable value of

$1 per share) they at the same time provide money market linked yields to clients. However, while 'retail MMMFs', which cater to small household investors, were the predominant investor type up to the late 1990s, after that point it was 'institutional MMMs' that cater to large investors such as corporations, pension funds and insurance companies, which became the predominant type (see Appendix B, Figure B.7). The major reason for the popularity of MMMFs with institutional investors is that, with the continuing growth in the volumes of cash held by them, MMMFs offered a convenient and economically efficient way of storing much of these volumes in a safe and liquid form.

The most striking outcome of the 'institutionalisation' of the MMMF client base is that changes in the overall size of MMMF sector as measured by its total assets began to exactly mirror the changes in the federal funds rate (down when the federal funds rate was down between 2002 and 2004 and sharply up between 2005 and 2007 when the federal funds rate was up), whereas there was absolutely no relation between that rate and US MMMF size prior to the early 2000s (see Appendix B, Figure B.8). The explanation for this new development is that institutional investor demand for MMMF services is far more sensitive to money market rates than is the demand exercised by household investors. For households, the relevant short-term asset choice is between bank deposits and MMMF holdings, and as long as the yields delivered by MMMFs exceed the interests on bank deposits, households will not withdraw funds from the MMMFs. By contrast, institutional investor cash deposits with MMMFs are highly interest elastic in that yield motives are as important here as are those to do with safe storage: thus, when short-term interest rates are low relative to long-term rates only those amounts deposited for storage purposes will register as the yield factor declines in importance, while extra amounts of cash stocks will be deposited over and above those for storage purposes when short-term rates are high relative to the long-term rates as institutional investors seek to take advantage of this yield differential.

Given the increased inflows of cash from institutional investors seeking to benefit from the rise in short-term yields after 2004, the MMMFs obviously had to find equivalent amounts of short-term securities to accommodate these inflows. Furthermore, given that US Treasury bills were in short supply due to the heavy influx of foreign government funds into these instruments, the MMMFs were forced to resort to short-term financial assets supplied by the private sector. Although MMMFs increased their overall holdings of commercial paper in the immediate pre-crisis period, it was the ABCP segment of the commercial paper market that was by far the most responsive to

MMMF demand. The US market for short-term commercial paper basically comprises three segments: those for financial commercial paper, non-financial commercial paper and ABCP. The ABCP segment is the youngest of the three, having, as stated, only been established in the 1980s. It also remained the smallest in size right up to the early 2000s when the situation started to change, first gradually as the ABCP segment began to match the other segments and then rapidly between the end of 2004 and mid-2007 when it became by this latter point in time the largest segment accounting for over 60% of all US commercial paper ($1.2 trillion out a total of $2 trillion; see Appendix B, Figure B.9). The reason why the other segments were less responsive is that the supplies of financial and non-financial commercial paper are ultimately determined not only by the amount of debt that the issuing bank and non-bank corporations wish to carry but also by the structure of that debt. In light of the continuing fall in long-term interest rates, while short-term rates continued to rise between mid-2004 and 2007, many fundraising corporations chose to lock into the low long-term rates by issuing more bonds and cutting back on their issuance of commercial paper. Thus, faced with an increasing shortage of financial and non-financial commercial paper relative to the amounts needed to accommodate their institutional clients' need for yield, the MMMFs had little option but to turn to the banking system, and to its conduits in particular, to make good the shortfall.

So great was the pace of demand for US ABCP from the end of 2004 onwards that US bank-owned conduits appeared to need a huge degree of help from foreign-bank owned conduits to cope with that demand. Of the $900 billion bank-conduit issued US ABCP outstanding in mid-2007, European banks accounted for about 60% of this amount, US banks for about 30% and Japanese banks for the remainder (see Appendix B, Figure B.10). Although no single European country's banks could match those of the USA in the rate of ABCP creation (see Appendix B, Figure B.11), it is nevertheless remarkable that the aggregate European percentage share of the US ABCP market by 2007 should have been substantially above that of the US banks when we consider that the contemporaneous European contribution to supplies of ABSs and CDOs was almost negligible: of the $11 trillion ABSs and $3 trillion CDOs outstanding in mid-2007 the European banking sector accounted for a mere 17% of both amounts.[3] One explanation for the discrepancy between the European banks' minor contribution to ABS and CDO issuance on the one hand and their major contribution to ABCP issuance on the other are the very different construction requirements needed by these different types of debt securities.

The short-term and typically non-tradable nature of ABCP means that these instruments are relatively easy to construct compared with ABSs, which, as long-term instruments, require more paperwork if they are to be capable of being traded away from the initial conditions of issuance. The difference in technical difficulty and complexity is even more pronounced in the case of CDOs given that the inclusion of securitised sub-prime mortgage loans in the mixture of backing collateral entails the use of sophisticated CETs to make these products in any way viable as investable assets. Thus, given the relative ease with which ABCP could be created, the European banks were well able to join with their US counterparts in accommodating the institutional demand for short-term paper when this demand began to expand rapidly from the end of 2004.

A further clue pointing to the primacy of institutional demand for yield in the sharp growth of the US ABCP market in the immediate pre-crisis period concerns the conduit programme breakdown of the market. As already noted, these programmes were broadly divided between those where credit loans formed the major collateral behind ABCP issuance and those where securities were the major backing collateral. It is noteworthy that where in 2002 the credit loan-backed programmes accounted for 77% of US ABCP then outstanding, by mid-2007 their percentage share had fallen to roughly 63%, while the share of the securities-backed programmes rose from 23% to 37% over the same period.[4] This development in a sense mirrored what was happening at the same time in the CDO market. Despite the high rate of supply of cash CDOs after 2002, this rate was still not enough to satisfy the rapid rise in demand for yield, which is why from about 2004 it was synthetic CDOs that became the dominant component of total CDO stocks ($2 trillion out of $3 trillion by mid-2007). Unlike cash CDOs, which could take months to be created because they require the physical involvement of household borrowers and of the commercial banks that lend to them in their creation, synthetic CDOs took only a few days to be established in that they involved nothing other than the use of credit default swaps. A similar situation appeared to arise in the ABCP market from about mid-2005 in that while the loan-backed programmes continued to carry the major burden of ABCP supply, the high rate of demand for these products combined with the limits to the amounts of loans that could be mustered as collateral in the time needed meant that securities-backed programmes, which could be launched more quickly, had to be called upon to help carry the burden.

In sum, the investor search for yield pressure was the principal force driving banks to buy CDOs as much as it was the principal force driving banks to supply CDOs. In the latter case, the pressure was direct: faced with an excess demand for ordinary, ground-floor US debt securities, the US banking sector had to expand the supply of first-floor ABSs, then the supply of second-floor CDOs and then, because of the limits on the rate of cash CDO creation, the supply of synthetic CDOs. In the former case, the pressure was indirect: having helped to force up US short-term interest rates through their contribution to the threat of US house price inflation caused in large part by the heavy increase in residential mortgage issuance necessitated by the need for collateral in ABS and CDO production, institutional investors then sought to take advantage of these short-term rates by buying the type of short-term commercial paper that only the banks could issue in the volumes demanded and, what is more, could only do so in part by using CDOs as collateral for this paper. In light of these different ways in which the CDO market was made to absorb the pressure of investors' search for yield, it is little wonder that the US and European financial sectors suffered so much damage when that market collapsed in the summer of 2007. The first group of institutions to be hit were the hedge funds that had been the major buyers of CDOs and the investment banks that had lent heavily to the hedge funds and had accepted CDOs as collateral. The next two groups were the insurance companies, which not only had insured the various tranches of the cash CDOs but had also participated heavily in the construction of synthetic CDOs in their role as protection sellers in CDO-linked credit default swaps, and the bank-owned or bank-sponsored conduits that had used CDOs as part of the collateral in their issuance of ABCP. The final, and by far the largest, group of institutions that suffered heavily from the sub-prime crisis were all those commercial banks – not only the US and UK banks, but also the Irish, Icelandic, Spanish and Portuguese banks – that had in the preceding period come to rely on a particular business model, namely, short-term borrowing at one set of rates in the money markets to finance long-term lending at another set of rates in various loan markets including the mortgage loan market. This model was safe as long as lenders had trust and confidence in the creditworthiness of the borrowing institutions and thus willing to lend at low rates, but became lethal when lenders lost that trust in the wake of the sub-prime crisis and either raised lending rates or withdrew short-term funding altogether.

4.4

To point to the global search for yield as the primary force that drove the banking sector to create CDOs on a scale sufficient to precipitate the crisis of 2007–8 is also to point to the causal primacy of inequality in that crisis. At the heart of the matter are the twinned aspects of the regressive side of the global commodity system's dynamic: the dispersion aspect, the increasingly uneven distribution of income and wealth across different groups of people, and the concentration aspect, the accumulation of increasing amounts of wealth in the hands of a tiny number of people, the world's HNWIs. Just as the dispersion aspect was critical to the supply-side factors driving CDO growth between 2003 and 2007, given that it was sub-prime and other nonconforming mortgage loans that formed the basic raw material needed for the construction of CDOs, and given that many of those who took out these loans belonged to the poorer end of the American population, so was the concentration aspect critical to the demand-side factors driving CDO growth, given that HNWIs' wealth holdings not only helped to lower the yield of highly rated traditional bond classes, which contributed to the emergence of the search for yield phenomenon, but also led to increasing assets being placed under the management of hedge funds who were the major buyers of CDOs. In expanding on these details, let us start with the role of the hedge funds.

The acceleration in CDO production between 2002 and 2007 was closely paralleled by a rapid growth of the hedge fund industry. Hedge fund assets more than tripled between 2002 and 2007, rising from US\$600 billion to about US\$2.2 trillion, while the number of firms operating within the industry doubled from about 5,000 to about 10,000 in this period (see Appendix B, Figure B.12). The key drivers behind the growth of the hedge fund industry were the increasing amounts of wealth of HNWIs, which was partly channelled into hedge funds, and the 'institutionalisation' of the hedge funds' client base. Institutional investments in hedge funds remained comparatively modest up to 2002, but after that date these investments rose rapidly, a central motivating factor being their search for yield (see Appendix B, Figure B.13). Faced with these large cash inflows from clients demanding yield, the hedge funds found that one of the most effective ways of meeting this demand was through investments in CDOs. By June 2007, hedge funds were the largest group of investors in CDOs, holding nearly half of all these products (around US\$1.4 trillion; see Appendix B, Figure B.14). In contrast to institutional asset managers, which had to severely restrict the amounts of the high-risk and unrated CDO equity tranches that they bought on account of prudential and regulatory constraints, hedge funds faced no such constraints in their involvement in the CDO market. This meant that they could go long on the risky equity tranches, thus enabling them to take advantage of their high yields while at the same time controlling for risk through the use of credit default swaps and put options. At the same time, they also held substantial amounts of the senior tranches that were used as collateral to leverage their clients' funds by a factor of around four. Both of these strategies allowed them to generate the 11% average returns that were given back to investors in 2006. To maximise gross returns on assets, the hedge funds had to maximise the net returns that had to be given back to these clients, while at the same time keeping the costs of borrowing the extra sums of money to a minimum. CDOs fitted into this equation supremely well. There were other securities, such as emerging market bonds, that gave high returns but could not be used as collateral in borrowing arrangements and there were other securities, such as US Treasuries, which could be used as collateral but gave poor returns. Only CDOs combined these two distinct advantages together, because only they comprised AAA-rated securities at one end of the scale with unrated equity securities at the other end.

In view of the increasing reliance on CDOs as a means by which hedge funds could generate yield for clients, it follows that HNWIs had to have been heavily implicated in CDO growth by virtue of having continued to increase their investments in hedge funds after 2002. The number of HNWIs was around 10 million in 2007, a figure that represented just 0.15% of the world's population of 6.6 billion. The supposition that these individuals could have had any significant impact in the US bond markets in the pre-sub-prime crisis era may seem incredible when one considers how small in number they were, but not when one considers the amounts of wealth that they concentrated in their hands and the forms in which this wealth was stored. In 2007, the world's HNWIs had approximately US$41 trillion in assets (world GDP in that year was $55 trillion) as compared with approximately $19 trillion in 1997. Prior to the crisis, HNWIs were the largest global investor group with more assets under management than global pension funds ($28 trillion), mutual funds ($26 trillion) and insurance companies ($20 trillion). Financial securities represented the most prominent form in which HNWIs stored their wealth, accounting for an average of 54% for the whole period from 2002 to 2007. Given that HNWI asset allocation to debt securities accounted for $11 trillion in 2007 (roughly 14% of the total global stock of debt securities in that year) and given the degree to which private investor demand influenced US bond yields, it seems that HNWIs must also have had a negative influence on yields by virtue of what can be called their 'blocking' role. Amounts of HNWI bond holdings were so substantial that had these amounts been available to all of the other types of investor it is doubtful whether the problem of yield would have become as acute as it did. The irony, however, is that, having helped to create the yield problem by virtue of channelling the bulk of their wealth into financial securities, the seriously rich individuals then continued to be an important source of the pressure on the hedge funds to find ways of resolving the problem. Although their percentage share of the total assets placed with hedge funds fell from 60% to just over 40% in the years preceding the financial crisis as money flowed in from other sources, HNWIs still remained by far the largest single group of hedge fund clients.

The reverse side of the huge accumulation of wealth in the hands of a few individuals was stagnant wage growth for the majority of the world's working population. Stagnant wages outside of the US, and particularly in Asia, were an additional contributory factor to the demand pull pressures behind the rapid growth of CDOs in the immediate pre-crisis era. The early 2000s witnessed a rapid expansion in foreign investment inflows into the US bond markets, with foreign governments investing primarily in US Treasury bonds for exchange rate management purposes and foreign private institutions and individuals investing in US municipal, corporate and agency (prime mortgage backed) bonds. While the relative shortage of domestic investable securities in the Asian and other emerging market economies meant that much of the large trade surpluses with the US had to be housed in US securities, the fact remains that an important part of the reason for these trade surpluses can be traced back to the constraints on domestic investments in the emerging market economies caused by low wages and corresponding consumption demand constraints.

Stagnant wages coupled with job insecurity in the US itself were central among the supply-side forces driving CDO growth, as was evidenced by the changes in the composition of residential mortgage loans, the raw material needed for the creation of ABSs and CDOs. These loans were broadly divided into two categories: conforming or prime agency loans, loans given to individuals with a good credit rating, and nonconforming loans, which in turn divided into jumbo loans (so called because they had an above-average loan to property value ratio), alternative-A loans (alt-A borrowers were just below prime borrowers in that, while having no income documentation, they had a good credit rating) and subprime loans (borrowers belonging to the subprime category either had no credit history or an extremely poor one and included NINAs, those with no income and no assets, and NINJAs, those with no income, no job and no assets). It is striking that while conforming residential mortgage loans comprised the majority of all such loans in the US right up to early 2004, between then and mid-2007 it was the nonconforming segment that became the majority part of such loans (see Appendix B, Figure B.15). What this fact points to is that the strength of investor demand for standard, prime-backed ABSs was so strong, but the limits to the amounts of creditworthy US households eligible for mortgage loans so tight, that the US banking sector had no option but to bring into the mortgage market the very poorest of the US working population. Of course, there were many of these people who had dreams of owning their own home, but the acceleration in sub-prime mortgage issuance from 2004 to mid-2007 had less to do with realising these dreams than with boosting the rate of supply of the raw material needed for the CDO production process.

The task of enticing large numbers of nonconforming borrowers into the mortgage market was principally achieved by offering adjustable rate mortgages (ARMs), i.e. mortgages that were initially set at a low percentage rate for a set period, typically a year, and then reset at a certain percentage above the federal funds rate. The task of transforming these nonconforming loans into structured securities acceptable to final-end investors was principally achieved through the use of the CETs described earlier. The contradiction is that the very same methods used to bring extra numbers of borrowers into the mortgage loan market and the very same techniques used to create extra volumes of mortgage-backed securities were also those that ensured both the inevitability of a financial crisis and the immensity of its destructive force. A continuing dependence on the extension of ordinary mortgage loans would have meant fewer borrowers but also fewer delinquencies once the federal funds rate began to rise from June 2004. As it was, the use of low entry cost ARMs, while succeeding in enticing large numbers of sub-prime borrowers into the mortgage market, also had as its flip side the problem that once they began to be reset at relatively high rates in the 2005–6 period, there were so many sub-prime borrowers defaulting at the same time that all of the safeguards built into the CDOs were breached. On the other side of the equation, had CDOs conformed with the same level of transparency as characterised all other debt securities, the rise in their risks due to the rise in the default rate could still have been monitored and priced. As it was, the various CETs used to create the CDOs caused them to be so opaque and complex that when the federal funds rate rose too high in too short a time span, thus causing the delinquency rate to overshoot all expectations, the market for CDOs simply disintegrated overnight. Indeed, the distrust in CDOs suddenly became so intense that, having ostensibly been created to spread risk in the financial sector, these products instead became instruments for spreading fear.

4.5

To summarise, the global financial crisis was in the end all about developments at the margin. Even at the height of its expansion in 2007,
the CDO market remained a comparatively small part of the global
financial sector, totalling $3 trillion as compared with the $67 trillion
government and corporate bond markets and the $11 trillion ABS
market, and yet its proportions were such as to have been able to cause
the financial sector to go into cardiac arrest that year. These proportions were not reached because of various failures within the financial sector. Absent those failures and the sector would still have come
close to collapse because of the extra weight it was forced to carry in
the same way that the world's strongest man, capable of lifting, say, a
world-record-breaking weight of 575 kg would come close to collapse
if forced to carry an extra 25 kg. The various weaknesses and lapses
on the part of the commercial banks and the other institutions linked
to them certainly facilitated the rapid growth of the CDO market between 2003 and 2007, but it was global inequality that provided the
all-encompassing causal framework for that growth. Had income and
wealth been more evenly distributed in the global economy, the pressures on the banking system to artificially inflate securities stocks and
thus their aggregate wealth storage capacity would have eased sufficiently so as not to force it into creating the toxic securities on the
scale that it did. The additional point is that, had there been a more
even distribution of income and wealth, there would have been greater
numbers of prime, creditworthy households eligible for mortgage
loans, thus relaxing the pressure on the banking system to supplement
those numbers with sub-prime borrowers. In short, it was the fact that
the scale of inequality generated by the newly operational global commodity system had rapidly become so great that caused its basic rules
to be broken, thus precipitating its first serious crisis.

Notes

1 The argument developed in this section and the data sources used are
   drawn from the following series of papers: Lysandrou (2011a, 2011b, 2013),
   Lysandrou and Nesvetailova (2015), Lysandrou and Shabani (2018), Goda
   et al. (2013) and Goda and Lysandrou (2014).
2 See Lysandrou and Shabani (2018).
3 See Goda and Lysandrou (2014).
4 See Ahern (2007).

5 Control

5.1

The cardinal lesson that falls out of the preceding analysis is that the regressive side of the global commodity system's dynamic has to be brought under tight control if another financial crisis such as that witnessed in 2007–8 is to be averted. To set the context for the type of control that will be proposed here, we begin with a brief look at two alternative sets of proposals: those advanced by mainstream economists, on the one hand, and those advanced by heterodox economists, on the other.

5.2

First established in the 1980s, dynamic stochastic general equilibrium (DSGE) models are now the major macroeconomic models used for policy guidance purposes by many central banks and by a number of international institutions. The name of these models points to the key premises that characterise their stylised representation of a modern-day economy: (i) that it comprises two groups of agents, households and firms, which generally formulate decisions regarding current and future consumption and investment expenditures in a rationally consistent manner; (ii) that all of these rational decisions and forward-looking expectations are geared to the attainment of well-defined goals, preference maximisation on the part of households and profit maximisation on the part of firms; (iii) that the attainment of these goals is subject to constraints, budget constraints for households and technological constraints for firms; (iv) that forward-looking optimising agents will quickly factor into their decisions the risks arising out of any external shocks to the economy, examples of such shocks being the introduction of new technologies, a change in the price of a key resource such as oil or a change in government policy; (v) finally, that the set of prices that holds at any particular moment is that which reconciles household and firm objectives subject to their budget and technological constraints and to the resource constraints of the entire economy.

From the outset of the financial crisis, DSGE models came under criticism for their failure to predict the crisis and thus to give proper and early guidance to policymakers as to what to do to prevent the crisis from rapidly escalating on the scale that it did. This criticism is misplaced in that the peculiarities of the crisis were such as to have made it virtually impossible for any macromodel, not matter how mathematically sophisticated, to have predicted it. Rather, the more appropriate criticisms that should be levelled against the whole DSGE paradigm pertain, first, to the type of explanations that those guided by it give to the root causes of the financial crisis, and second, to the type of policy lessons drawn from those explanations.

As CDOs were at the epicentre of the global financial crisis, any account of that crisis must explain how the market for these toxic securities came to grow to a size sufficiently large enough to wreak havoc went it collapsed. Recall that in the explanation given earlier, the demand-side factors in CDO market growth were given as much as attention as the supply-side factors. By contrast, it is only these latter factors that have been highlighted by most mainstream economists. One reason for this disparity is that the core assumptions of their macroeconomic models make no allowance for exploitation. In the two-space perspective on global production presented earlier, it was argued that the global volume of material output produced at any time must be mapped into commodity space as a global expanse of values (outputs whose physical qualities and hence whose prices are judged against social standards); that all individuals involved in the global commodity system occupy, by virtue of that involvement, both opposing positions with respect to the global value expanse (i.e. they all contribute to the creation of that expanse by virtue of their power of sanction over prices while at the same time they all subtract a proportion of that expanse according to the type and amount of commodities in their possession); that while the majority of individuals who only possess their labour power subtract a relatively small proportion from that global expanse there is a tiny number of individuals who can subtract a relatively large proportion because of their possession of multiple types and amounts of income-generating commodities; finally, that it was the need for financial securities on the part of these rich individuals as a means of storing their accumulating amounts of wealth that formed part of the demand-pull pressure on the banking system to create extra stocks of investable assets.

In contrast to all of this, mainstream macroeconomic models strip out the qualitative (i.e. social standard-based) determinants of outputs and prices and focus only on the quantitative determinants: the aggregate amount of material outputs produced in an economy at any given time is determined by the volume of resources available to that economy and by the state of technology; firms alone appear on the production side of outputs while households appear on the consumption side (some households may appear on the production side insofar as they supply labour to firms, but those that do not are excluded from the production side); prices in this context are only socially determined in the sense that they adjust up and down to reconcile technology-constrained supplies of outputs with the budget-constrained demands for them; as prices adjust according to the law of demand and supply as much in the markets for factor inputs as in the markets for final outputs, there can be no exploitation and surplus appropriation anywhere in the system, from which it in turn follows that there can be no pressure of demand for extra amounts of financial securities to help store the accumulating amounts of surplus wealth.

The failure to acknowledge that surplus appropriation and wealth accumulation added to the problem of a global excess demand for securities as stores of value leads to the more general reason why the majority of mainstream economists have paid no attention to the demand side of the CDO market. This is that the very problem of an excess demand for securities simply cannot arise in their macroeconomic models. In the two-space perspective advanced earlier, it was argued that financial securities have now become commodities in their own right because of the transformation of asset management into a mass industry and because of the corresponding rise in institutional investor demand for investables. As in the product markets, excess demand and supply problems can arise in the securities markets, but the equilibrating mechanism for resolving them here is necessarily different. In product markets the imbalances between supplies and demands can notionally be resolved through price adjustments: prices up when there are excess demands and prices down when there are excess supplies. By contrast, price adjustments are not equilibrating in the securities markets that are now dominated by institutional and other large investors on the buy side. As securities have no intrinsic value, and as, therefore, it is through their prices alone that they can possess a quantitative, value storage property, it follows that investors generally need these prices to be stable over time if securities are to function as investables. Thus, if an excess demand for securities as stores of value emerges, the solution to the problem cannot be through a price adjustment process, as this would undermine their value storage property and would thus be self-defeating, but must instead be through a quantity adjustment process: more securities need to be supplied to soak up the excess demand, thereby keeping their prices and yields stable and thus their value storage property secure.

Now let us return to mainstream macroeconomic theory. The chief consequence of the fact that it only recognises two private sector groups of agents, firms and households, is that it only recognises the flow dimension of financial securities as being significant. As households do not market asset portfolios to the public as do pension funds and other institutional investors, they have no reason to treat securities as portable value containers into which clients' monies are poured and from which monies are extracted to repay clients and thus no reason to view securities differently from the way that they are viewed by firms: just as firms borrow funds for investment purposes on the promise to repay the funds at some point in the future, households lend funds in the expectation of being repaid those funds with an added return that can be used to finance future consumption. Households can choose between bank-based and security market-based forms of saving, but as they have no public asset management function, there is nothing preventing them from channelling all of their savings into bank deposits should the returns here be more favourable than are those on securities. This is in stark contrast to the constraint on institutional investors who must at all times keep the bulk of the assets under their management in the form of tradable securities.

The upshot of this is that as there are no agents in mainstream macroeconomic models who are concerned with the quantitative, value storage dimension of securities and who thus need securities prices to be stable so as to safeguard this quantitative dimension, these models see prices as performing the same equilibrating role in the securities markets as they do in the product markets. If, for example, households seek better returns from securities than are available on their bank deposits, their prices will go up and yields go down, thus encouraging firms to issue more securities to finance investment: in short, demand creates its own supply. Conversely, to take another example, if firms issue more securities for investment purposes than are currently demanded, their prices will have to fall and yields rise so as entice the required extra household demand for securities: in short, supply creates its own demand. As excess demands for securities can never be more than a fleeting phenomenon due to the equilibrating role of prices, it follows that the demand side of the securities markets can never be a source of pressure on the banking sector to create extra quantities of ABSs to compensate for any shortfall in the supplies of debt securities issued by corporations.[1] What of course then follows from viewing the financial crisis of 2007–8 through this particular lens is that all of the inducements and all of the pressures that led the US and European banking sectors to create the amounts of ABSs on the scale that they did must have come entirely from the supply side of the securities markets. In addition to the US commercial banks which used residential mortgage loans as the principal raw material in the creation of ABSs and CDOs, the other two major groups that were held to have been key to the expansion in supply of these securities were US households who took out these mortgage loans in the first place and the US government that encouraged the securitisation of these loans as a means of expanding US home ownership.

According to mainstream analyses, the common factor behind each of these groups' contribution to the financial crisis was a gross undervaluation of risk. In the case of the household sector there were simply too many US households who readily took out mortgage loans that they could not afford to service. While mainstream macroeconomists make no allowance for exploitation and surplus extraction, some recognise that the processes of globalisation and rapid technological change, among other factors, have led to widening inequality as those individuals with fewer educational qualifications are less able to cope with these developments compared with those who have better qualifications and who are thus less exposed to the twin threats of unemployment and stagnant wage growth. The conclusion that then comes out of this line of argument is that as the poorer individuals still had the same aspirations as had the richer ones of home ownership they found that the easiest way of filling the gap between those aspirations and the realities of low income and job insecurity was to take out mortgage debt. In the case of the banking sector, two main lines of argument have been advanced for its pre-crisis undervaluation of risk. One is that the period of the 'great moderation' (i.e. the unusual combination of steady growth with low rates of unemployment and inflation) spanning the early 1990s to the mid-2000s may have led banks to drop their guard and lend to households who on any close inspection were evidently in no position to service their debt. The other major line of argument highlights the profits made by banks from engaging in regulatory arbitrage, i.e. taking mortgage loans off their balance sheets where the costs of capital cover were high and passing them on to their off-balance-sheet vehicles where such costs were either minimal or absent altogether. Finally, in the case of the US government, the problem here according to mainstream economists essentially came down to a combination of overdependence on the private banking sector to meet household home ownership aspirations with under-regulation of that sector.[2] The US government, it has been argued, should have either made direct financial provision for expanding home ownership to the poorer US households or not encouraged those households to have home ownership aspirations, but what it especially should not have done is encourage those aspirations while trusting the banking sectors' assurances that it could meet those aspirations and at the same time manage the risks involved.

While the aforementioned storyline undoubtedly formed part of the explanation for the growth of the US ABS markets in the period prior to the financial crisis, it cannot provide the whole explanation as indicated by the distinctive peculiarities of that growth. Had the widespread undervaluation of risk on the part of the household, banking and government sectors been the central driving force behind the growth of the US ABS and CDO markets, one would have expected to see that growth describe a higher trend rate of increase over a longer stretch of time than was actually the case. Rather, the sudden and extremely sharp acceleration in the rate of growth of these markets from 2004 through to mid-2007, combined with the fact that this acceleration exactly coincided with the acceleration in the rate of increase of foreign and domestic investor demand for US yield-bearing securities, would indicate that it was this demand that was the principal driver behind the growth of the ABS and CDO markets in the immediate pre-crisis era. Further confirmation that this was the case as regards the CDO market in particular is provided by the fact that from early 2005 onwards it was synthetic CDOs – i.e. CDOs that did not require the physical involvement of mortgage borrowing households or mortgage lending banks in their construction but which simply took cash CDOs as their underlying reference entities in credit default swaps – that constituted the dominant component of total CDO issuance.

It could be that the reason why mainstream theorists have tended to downplay or ignore altogether the role played by investor demand for yield in the financial crisis is that to admit the centrality of that role is to admit the possibility that the fault lines at the root of the crisis had more to do with structural flaws in the contemporary economic system than with behavioural failures on the part of particular groups of individuals and organisations. Be that as it may, what is certain is that the singling out of the undervaluation of risk as having been at the root of the pre-crisis growth of the US ABS and CDO markets has had serious and potentially very damaging policy implications. A central thrust of post-crisis policy has been to tighten the various rules and regulations in the financial sector to ensure that all of its participants properly assess and price the risks that they take on. This initiative implemented on its own would be entirely justified if it could be safely assumed that a global demand for yield-bearing securities could never again recur on a scale that would require the US banking sector to create extra volumes of ABSs to satisfy this demand. However, no such assumption can be made. Having temporarily dipped in the immediate aftermath of the financial crisis, the volume of global asset demand has again resumed its upward growth path and the irony is that it has done so in some part because of the side effects of the expansionary monetary policies aimed at tackling the fallout of the crisis. With central bank interest rates in the major economies set to remain unusually low in the foreseeable future, mid- to high income households will continue to place more and more of their savings with asset managers in the search for higher returns, and as they do so, asset managers will have to purchase more and more securities in order to accommodate their clients' needs. Furthermore, in addition to the stimulus given to institutional investor demand for securities, there is also the stimulus given to the demand stemming from the very rich individuals who, benefitting from the boost to their wealth given by the low interest rate boost to asset prices, seek to capitalise on this benefit by accumulating even more yield-bearing assets.

Now, if, on the one hand, tighter regulation of mortgage and other credit lending restricts the rate of supply of ABSs, and if, on the other hand, looser monetary policy stimulates the rate of demand for yield-bearing securities to the point where that rate exceeds the rate at which governments and corporations can issue their own debt securities, then it follows that the excess demand for securities must find vent in a market for structured financial securities. That market may not be a CDO market where sub-prime mortgage loans form part of the backing collateral but something more like the market for collateralised loan obligations where corporate junk bonds are a major part of the collateral. However, the dangers in relying on high-risk debt instruments to artificially inflate securities stocks are just as high. In sum, having failed to identify the global excess demand for securities as one of the root causes of the last great financial crisis, the financial regulators and central banks based in the world's leading economies seem to be doing their best to ensure that an excess demand for securities will again reach such proportions as can cause the next great financial crisis.

5.3

While the policy responses to the financial crisis advanced by heterodox economists are generally different from those advanced by mainstream economists, their analyses of the causes of the crisis are in some respects very similar.[3] The similarities pertain above all to the fact that heterodox theorists do not see a global excess demand for securities as having been a major driving force behind the growth of the toxic securities that triggered the crisis. One reason for this is that heterodox macroeconomic models do not allow for exploitation and an accumulation of surplus wealth that then needs to be housed in income-generating assets. There are those on the orthodox Marxist wing of heterodoxy who do single out exploitation and surplus appropriation as being the distinguishing features of capitalist economies, but as this is a restrictive view of exploitation, inasmuch as it traces the locus of exploitation in class relations in the production realm, it remains very much a minority view. The other, and more general, reason for the heterodox exclusion of an excess demand for securities as a causal factor in the crisis is the exclusion in heterodox macroeconomic models of the institutional asset management industry as a distinct sector in its own right.

Consider, by way of example, post-Keynesian stock-flow models, now generally considered to be the most advanced and comprehensive type of heterodox macroeconomic model. These models take the aggregate sector rather than the rational choice maximising agent as their basic unit of analysis, the five main sectors being firms, households, banks, government and the central bank. Institutional asset managers are subsumed under the household sector, but as households have no reason to view financial securities differently from the way that they are viewed by corporate issuers, it follows that it is only the capacity of securities as financing instruments that is of importance in these models. Securities may serve as parts of the stocks from which funds flow at the start of a given period and to which funds return at the end of that period, but in between these two points in time, securities are not thought to serve as portable investables, assets whose stock dimension, i.e. value storage capacity, is as important throughout the trading period as it is at the beginning and at the end of that period. As a consequence of the omission of an institutional investor perspective on securities, post-Keynesian macromodels end up depicting the financial markets as the one group of markets that operate to an equilibrating price adjustment rule rather than to a quantity adjustment rule.[4] Thus, to repeat the point previously made in regard to mainstream theory, as excess demands for securities in post-Keynesian theories can never be more than a temporary phenomenon due to the equilibrating role of prices, it follows that the demand side of the securities markets can never be a source of pressure on the banking sector to create extra quantities of ABSs to compensate for any shortfall in the supplies of debt securities issued by corporations.

When turning to heterodox explanations of the supply-side factors that were held to drive the pre-crisis growth of the markets for CDOs and other ABSs, we find that even here there are certain overlaps with the mainstream explanations. Heterodox economists agree that the US government should not have entrusted the programme for expanding home ownership to the private banking sector, but then go further and argue that this line of policy was entirely consistent with the neo-liberal doctrine, reinforced by the current vintage of mainstream macroeconomic theory, that economic efficiency is maximised when government intervention in the market economy is minimised. Similarly, while agreeing that the banks stood to profit from engaging in regulatory arbitrage, heterodox economists then go further in arguing that the marked shift away from the traditional 'originate and hold' model of mortgage lending, which forced banks to closely monitor the risks on the mortgage loans that they extended, towards the 'originate and distribute' model, which allowed banks to relax their risk controls as a consequence of mortgage loans being taken off their balance sheets, was entirely consistent with the neo-liberal doctrine that security-market-based forms of finance are more cost efficient than are the traditional bank-based forms.

As concerns the role of the US household sector in the financial crisis, while there is agreement that the poorer households were encouraged to rely on debt to realise their home ownership aspirations, the difference between the heterodox position on this issue and that of the mainstream pertains not only to a critique of the neo-liberal ideology that gave this encouragement but also, and more crucially, to the explanation of what lies behind the continuing rise in inequality between households. Where those in the mainstream single out as a key factor education-related differences in the ability to cope with the effects of globalisation and rapid technological change, heterodox economists go on to add this what is considered to be at present an even more important casual factor behind rising inequality. This is the financialisation of the world economy, by which is meant the ongoing growth in the size and weight of the world's financial markets relative to the world's product markets.

It was previously argued that the expansion of the securities markets relative to the material product base, made possible by the extension of the commodity principle to debt and equity securities, facilitates exploitation and ensuing inequality both by helping to compress the wage share in the global value expanse and by helping to provide accommodation to surplus wealth accumulation. By contrast, the general position of heterodox theorists is not just that financialisation facilitates inequality but also that it causes inequality just as financialisation is itself in turn caused by inequality. Industrial profit is the key variable in this relation of mutual causality, the logic being as follows: firms under capitalism usually produce in order to generate profit, an aim which in turn can only be fully realised if household wage incomes and hence money-backed demand for consumption goods are maintained at a commensurable level; on the contrary, if wage incomes and hence the aggregate level of effective demand lag behind aggregate profits, thus placing constraints on the proportion of profits that can be realised in the normal way in the course of the production-consumption cycle, then firms will need to seek supplementary outlets through which profits can be realised, outlets that can be temporarily provided by the financial sector. Thus, the financialisation process, on this view, is essentially an anomaly, a dysfunctional outgrowth of capitalism whose sole purpose in continuing to unfold is to accommodate unproductive, speculative activities on a scale that can compensate for the limits on the scale of productive actives. But just as financialisation grows out of the constraints in production imposed by inequality, so also does its self-serving speculative nature cause further inequality inasmuch as it increasingly diverts jobs and resources away from the productive sector and towards financial services. The contradiction here, which explains why the whole financialisation process is considered to be in the end unsustainable, is that, by continually diverting resources away from the production sector in order to feed finance, financialisation is in effect eating away at its own foundations.

For heterodox theorists the financial crisis of 2007–8 was ultimately nothing other than the latest manifestation of the unsustainability of financialisation. In other words, contrary to the position advanced earlier that the root cause of the crisis was that the financial markets were too small inasmuch as the supply of financial securities could not keep up with the pace of demand, the general heterodox position is that the crisis happened because the financial markets had simply become too big. The policy conclusion that logically follows on from this diagnosis is that if future financial crises on the scale of the last one are to be avoided, action needs to be taken now to tackle financialisation. By this is meant not merely a programme for tightening the rules and regulations covering particular groups of agents involved in the financial

sector, as is the mainstream position, but a far more ambitious programme for 'de-financialisation'; that is to say, a programme aimed
not merely at controlling the rate of growth of the financial sector but
also at reversing that growth so as to eventually downsize the whole
sector and thereby make it fit for the purpose for which it was created
in the first place, namely, to serve the interests of the real sector.

The basic explanation for this heterodox position on finance is that
there continues to be a fixed view as to exactly how the financial sector
is supposed to serve the real sector and as to the exact quantitative
proportions that it needs to assume in order to perform that service.
As concerns the nature of finance's role, the heterodox standpoint
essentially coincides with that of mainstream finance theory, which
is that it is "to facilitate the allocation and deployment of economic
resources across time and space in an uncertain environment".[5] Where
mainstream and heterodox theorists diverge is over the appropriate
scale that finance needs to acquire to be able to facilitate the allocation and deployment of economic resources: the former argue that the
larger is the financial sector the more cost effectively can it carry out
its services in support of resource allocation, while the latter object to
this argument on the grounds that although the financial sector has to
reach a minimum scale in order to operate effectively its current scale
is far in excess of that minimum. The financial sector is held to be
bloated and this supposition, coupled with the fact that the sector cannot exist independently of the real sector, is generally taken to indicate
role reversal: rather than finance serving the interests of production, it
is production serving the interests of finance. Nowhere is this apparent
excess of financial scale and role reversal seen to be more pronounced
than in the trading sphere inasmuch as trading volumes in the securities
markets and other financial markets have in recent decades increased
at rates far above the trading volumes for material outputs or industrial investments. While it is conceded that some of this trading may
be linked to real sector activities, the fact that such trading constitutes
a vanishingly small fraction of total financial trading volumes coupled
with the observation that the latter are overwhelmingly dominated
by short horizon trades would appear to confirm the heterodox view
that the key financial trading motive is speculation: trading solely in
order to gain from trading. This identification of all short-term trading as purely speculative trading in turn explains why one the most
favoured tools for achieving de-financialisation is a tax on all financial
transactions.

There is no question that the financial sector's rationale is to serve
the interests of the real sector. What is in question is whether these

interests are solely to do with the efficiency with which economic resources are allocated and deployed. If this is the case then it must indeed follow that there is currently too much finance. However, this is not so. If the financial sector has grown in recent decades, and will continue to grow in the coming decades, it is because it must now serve a second purpose in addition to facilitating the efficiency of production in the real economy and that is to facilitate the financing of the capacities for production deployed in that economy. The point bears repeating that now that governments and corporations have a large and permanent need of security market forms of funding, they need institutional investors to be dominant on the buy side of the markets, investors who have liabilities on a scale and of a maturity such that match the assets issued by the borrowing organisations. However, alongside this need for an increased rate of institutional investor demand for securities must come acceptance of an accompanying increased rate of securities trading.

If institutional asset managers have to buy securities in large volumes because of the transformation of their industry into a mass industry, so does the shift towards standardised forms of asset management provision concomitant on that transformation explain why they have to engage in frequent trading. The fact that their portfolios typically follow a particular investment rule or style as laid down in a fund prospectus or investment mandate means that these portfolios must be constantly rebalanced if they are to be kept to their terms of reference while at the same time accepting new inflows of cash from clients or disbursing cash to clients. The fact that rebalancing trades are short term on account of their frequency may cause them to appear to be speculative in nature, but they are in reality the exact antithesis of speculative trades: for where speculative vehicles such as hedge funds trade to exploit any price disturbances in the securities markets, asset managers who need to trade for portfolio balancing purposes must do so in ways that avoid causing price disturbances so as to contain the costs of trading.

The upshot of this line of argument is that a strategy for definancialisation that involves as a first step an indiscriminate restriction of all short-term financial transactions will restrict the ability of institutional investors to absorb the amounts of securities that governments and corporations wish to issue, thus placing a restriction on these organisations' ability to spread their financial liabilities across different intervals in the future. In the case of governments this restriction would be particularly onerous given the increasing financial demands made upon them arising out of demographic change and other mounting pressures on domestic economies. There is scope for substantially increasing the amounts of tax revenues that governments can generate (more on this later), but given the continuing increase in the scale of demands on their various services, there would still remain significant gaps in their budgets. Now, if governments are prevented from issuing different dated bonds in the volumes required to bridge these gaps, they will have no alternative but to make extensive expenditure cuts. While most people would feel the effects of these cuts to one degree or other, it is the poorest people who cannot supplement any state provided services with their own private welfare arrangements that will suffer the most.

In sum, a strategy for de-financialisation, which is in essence a strategy for closing down the future as a repository where borrowing institutions can deposit their liabilities, will more likely intensify rather than reduce inequality. This is not all, for not only will this strategy achieve nothing, but it will also get in the way of strategies that can achieve something, such as one that prioritises a comprehensive tax on financial wealth rather than a blanket tax on financial transactions. The point is that any programme for stopping and possibly reversing the growth of the world's securities markets at a time when the majority of these markets remain tiny compared with the US markets and thus subject to the gravitational pull of the US dollar will only serve to further enhance the power of the dollar. In other words, a strategy for de-financialisation would be tantamount to unilateral disarmament in the face of dollar hegemony. Hardly ideal even when the US presidency is in the hands of a considerate and responsible individual, this course of action becomes positively dangerous when the presidency falls into the hands of someone who is decidedly lacking in any of these qualities.

5.4

Everything that has been said thus far points inexorably to the need for a global tax authority (GTA), that is to say, a supranational body that is composed of tax experts nominated by the world's national governments and that is vested with the power of authority in the realm of taxation. As society is far from ready to move onto a different organisational principle, the current global commodity system must be allowed to operate as a complete entity. However, as it operates in a way that continually reduces the share of world income and wealth accruing to the majority of the world's population while continually expanding the share accruing to a small number of individuals, developments which taken in conjunction can only lead to recurrent crises, it follows that some form of coordinated control over the global commodity system has to be established. This requirement entails the creation of new institutions through which that control can be exercised. Several such institutions will be required down the line, but if for reasons of expediency we must begin with just one institution, then it must be a GTA.

A GTA should have two major functions. The first is to put some order into the world's tax affairs. These are at present in a chaotic state, not only because different governments are operating very different tax systems but also because there are many jurisdictions where there is no meaningful tax system in place at all. The result of this chaos is very substantial financial losses to governments given the ability of large corporations and wealthy individuals to exploit the differences between national tax systems so as to minimise their tax liabilities. Were these losses to governments to be recouped through a global co-ordination of tax arrangements, the positive impact on jobs and wages would be significant as there could be far more government expenditures on a whole range of projects and services whose unprofitable nature preclude or at least inhibit private investment expenditures. Of course, any attempt at a coordination of national tax regimes through the offices of a GTA would be resisted by many governments on the grounds that such an initiative would undermine their sovereignty. The present situation in the European Union highlights the degree to which national governments are reluctant to cede their authority over tax affairs to a higher body, for while in just about every other area of policy, from the economic to the social to the environmental to the diplomatic and so on, there is a collective pooling of initiatives and priorities across the EU – and in the eurozone this even includes a pooling of authority over monetary policy – taxation remains the one policy area where there are minimal attempts at coordination. In response to the standard objection that tax coordination would interfere with a national government's sovereignty, the answer must be that in a highly integrated global economy where the blocking role of national borders only seriously applies to the masses of working individuals and small businesses and not to the super-rich individuals and large corporations, the exercise of one government's sovereignty over taxation undermines another government's sovereignty over taxation.

The second major function of a GTA must be to impose a global wealth tax, that is to say, a tax that would target the world's HNWIs and in particular the 'ultra'-HNWIs, those with net asset holdings of $30 million and above. In the eight years between 2007 and 2015, during which time much of the world's population suffered the effects of the financial crisis and bore the brunt of the austerity measures, many of which had resulted from government-financed bank bail-outs, the world's HNWI population had risen from 10 million to 15 million while their combined wealth had risen from about $41 trillion to close to $59 trillion.[6] Even more astounding than these figures is the remarkable degree to which the bulk of HNWI assets has come to be concentrated at the very top of the wealth pyramid, for in 2015 no less than 34% of the $59 trillion worth of assets accumulated that year, i.e. about $20 trillions' worth, was held by just 145,000 ultra-HNWIs. An average rate of return of 10% on this $20 trillion would have meant that this tiny number of super-rich individuals would have generated an aggregate income in 2015 that would have matched the GDP of India, a country with 1.3 billion people. A more conservatively esti-mated rate of return of 5% would still have meant that these 145,000 individuals earned an aggregate income in 2015 that would have been about as much as the GDP of Russia, a country with a population of 145 million people. The upshot is that, even if set at a modest rate, a global wealth tax imposed on the ultra-HNWIs to begin with could generate billions of dollars that could be put to a number of socially important uses. One example is the establishment of a global reserve fund that could be called upon in the event of natural disasters that are now happening with increasing frequency and whose financial conse-quences are severest for the poorest nations of the planet.

Any attempt at taxing the wealth of the rich will inevitably be met with several lines of fierce resistance. One line will be through the force of argument. A typical argument is that private wealth accu-mulation is merited insofar as it is the result of marked differences in individual ability, talent or work ethic. That this argument is largely wrong is shown by comparing the differences between individuals that obtained 50 years ago, say, with the differences that obtain today. There were, at that point in time, the same differences separating the top bankers and corporate managers from their employees, the top innovators from those with modest creative skills, the top sports, film and other types of personalities from the run-of-the-mill individuals belonging to their fields and so on, but there were then nothing like the same huge differences in income generation and wealth accumulation. If the income and wealth gaps separating the top ranks of individuals from the remaining ranks have grown enormously in the recent period, this is not because of any enormous growth of the differences in ability or talent but because of the enormous growth of the global value ex-panse. Given that all individuals active in the global commodity system contribute to that value expanse through their power of sanction over prices, it follows that it is only right that a proportionate share of the vast amounts subtracted from that socially sanctioned value expanse by the world's super-rich individuals be given back to society.

A further argument that is typically used to counter the case for a wealth tax is that as the number of super-rich individuals in whose hands are concentrated much of the accumulating volumes of wealth is so small, there can be no serious threat to the global economic system whatever the scale of that wealth concentration. This type of argument has recently been buttressed by the claim that wealth concentration played no causal role in the financial crisis of 2007–8. If all this were true, then it would be difficult to justify a global wealth tax other than on moral grounds, which, for all their worth, cannot on their own constitute a strong enough base from which to mount an all-out drive to implement such a tax.[7] However, none of this is true. Given the limits to the available supplies of other types of assets in which privately accumulated wealth can be stored, the majority portion of that wealth has to be stored in the form of financial securities, and this can pose serious problems to the functioning of the global economic system as attested by the contribution made by the super-rich to the global excess demand for securities that led to the creation of CDOs on a scale sufficient to trigger the financial crisis of 2007–8.

Another line of resistance to a global wealth tax would be through the force of political power. As things stand, the world's rich individuals led by the top 145,000 ultra-HNWIs have the world in their political grip. In some countries the billionaires and multimillionaires occupy many of the top positions and offices of state; in other countries they control the politicians through the financing of party organisations or through the control of the media through whose channels they can heavily influence electoral outcomes; and in yet other countries they control the actions of incumbent politicians by holding up to them the possibilities of being richly rewarded with consultancy positions, board directorships and other lucrative posts upon retirement from political office. This is not to deny that there are politicians who are genuinely independent and genuinely motivated to pursue distributive policies that can benefit the majority of their electorate. However, as experience has repeatedly shown, any attempt by any one government to impose a wealth tax without first winning the agreement and support of other governments is bound to fail, as the very wealthy are highly mobile and will do everything possible to escape such a tax. If a meaningful wealth tax is to become reality, there has to be a coordinated move towards the establishment of a GTA endowed with the power to implement and monitor such a tax, and the problem here, as we say, is that the world's rich individuals control enough political posts and enough politicians in enough countries as to ensure that that move will face substantial difficulties.

These difficulties, however, are not insurmountable because some of the same developments accompanying the emergence of a global commodity system that have served to enhance the concentration of political power in the hands of a wealthy few have also served to enhance the ability of the world's majority to challenge and overturn that concentration. Recall the observation that the massive size asymmetries separating countries as commodity masses in global commodity space find their reflection in the equally massive differences in the international currency status of national currencies; thus, the US dollar, which accounts for 44% of the $5 trillion daily turnover in the forex markets, has over 90 other national currencies in its orbit while the euro, which accounts for 23% of daily forex turnover, has some 25 other national currencies tied to it. The upshot of this observation is that were the governments of just these two currency jurisdictions to be won over to the proposal for a GTA it would not be too difficult to win the support of most of the other governments. A further development consequent on the emergence of a global commodity system as an operational totality, which can also help with the promotion of a campaign for a GTA, is the ascendency of the English language to a position of supremacy as the world's language of international communication. English has long been a major world language along with other such languages as Spanish or French, but if it has recently moved to a position of overall supremacy, as attested by the fact that speakers of other native languages are often forced to speak English in the course of their international transactions while the converse is not true for native speakers of English, this is not only because of globalisation, the closer integration of regional economies in the global commodity system, but also because of financialisation, the growing size and weight of the financial component of that system. The point here is that just as English in its capacity as a language of international communication facilitates wealth concentration through its facilitation of the growth and integration of the material product and financial securities markets, so also can English, by virtue of this same capacity, help to facilitate a campaign for taxing that wealth.

All this said, the success of any campaign for a GTA charged with the dual functions of tax regime coordination and wealth tax implementation comes down in the end to a ranking of priorities. The current range of policy objectives pursued by different groups of people in different countries is extremely wide and, what is more, it is getting wider by the day. There is no doubt that many of these objectives are very important indeed. There is equally no doubt that their realisation is in most cases contingent on extensive funding and that, in many of these cases, it is the government sector that has to be relied upon as the key source of funding. Thus, it follows that while there can be many policy objectives that are on a par in terms of social or moral importance, there is one policy objective that has to be ranked first in order of priority if the others are to have any chance of being funded to the degree necessary for their realisation. That policy objective is the establishment of a GTA. Just as the world's financial and political elites will make it their overriding priority to prevent the establishment of a GTA, so also must all those of billions of people who want a fairer and more equitable world make the establishment of a GTA their overriding priority.

5.5

The great financial crisis of 2007–8 was not at root a crisis of the global financial sector. The pressures of the newly emergent global commodity system may have found vent through that sector, but their source was to be found in the deeper structural imbalances of the global commodity system. Those imbalances are all ultimately bound up with the fact that the system operates in a way that continually squeezes the share of the world's income and wealth that goes to the majority of the world's population, thereby allowing a continual accumulation of wealth in the hands of a small minority of individuals. The conclusion that falls out of all this is that any attempt to prevent future financial crises by regulating financial institutions and their practices and products while leaving untouched the continuing process of surplus appropriation and wealth concentration will not only not succeed in this attempt but will, if anything, make future financial crises even more likely. Just as counterproductive, if for different reasons, is a strategy that aims to prevent future financial crisis by downsizing the entire financial sector. Certain dysfunctional aspects of contemporary finance undoubtedly need to be stripped away and suppressed, but to indiscriminately target all financial markets, all financial institutions and all financial practices for suppression is a programme that will aggravate, rather than alleviate, the structural inequalities in the global commodity system and thus will make future financial crises more, rather than less, likely. The only way to avoid financial crises on the scale of the last one is to allow the global commodity system to continue to operate as a complete totality while at the same time controlling for the regressive side of that system's operational dynamic. A GTA will not go more than a little way in achieving this aim. It nevertheless represents a point of entry, an opening initiative that, if nursed through every stage of opposition and resistance, may lay the foundation for further initiatives that can in the end reverse the inequalities in income and wealth distribution that have now reached obscene proportions. There are no reasons why this modern world of ours should be one of stark contrasts, with a few thousands of individuals at one end of the spectrum disposing of vast amounts of wealth while billions of people at the other end must survive on scraps and remnants. No reasons at all. None.

Notes

1 Some mainstream economists did point to global investor demand for US debt securities as having been key to the financial crisis (see e.g. Caballero, 2010). However, this position has not gained widespread support because of the entrenched view that it is only the 'flow' ('yield') dimension of securities that matters. Thus, Claudio Borio, chief economist at the BIS, recently dismissed the argument that an excess demand for safe assets was an important factor in the financial crisis on the grounds that

> strong demand for safe assets in the run-up to the Great Financial Crisis should have led to a widening, not a narrowing, of the spread between safe and risky assets. Associating this demand for safe assets with a search for yield is misleading, since higher demand for safety points to higher, not lower, risk aversion or risk perceptions.
> (Borio, 2014, p. 15)

The phrase 'safe asset' is here interpreted to mean an entity that is certain to generate a return rather than also as an entity that preserves its value storage capacity over time. From a purely flow or yield perspective, Borio is right to say that the demand for 'safe assets' means that there should have been a widening of yield spreads in the run-up to the crisis, as risk averse investors would have needed more inducement to buy high-risk securities such as CDOs. From a stock perspective, however, Borio is wrong: if what ultimately matters to large investors is the value storage capacities of securities as much as their yields, it follows that when the supply of 'safe' stores of value cannot keep pace with investor demand the resulting excess demand must be directed to less safe value containers. When institutional investors were buying CDOs in large quantities in the run-up to the crisis, they surely wanted yield, but they also just as surely wanted the extra amounts of investables in which to store their wealth.

2 See e.g. Rajan (2010).

3 This section draws on Lysandrou (2011c, 2013a, 2016).

4 Thus, to quote Godley and Lavoie, "market clearing through prices does not usually occur except in financial markets" (2012, p. 18). See Lysandrou (2014b) for further discussion.
5 Merton and Brodie (1995, p. 4).
6 Capgemini (2016).
7 Thomas Piketty concludes his 2014 book *Capital in the Twenty-First Century* with a call for a global wealth tax. His case for such a tax is strong, but it would have been made stronger had he shown how the steep rise in economic inequality had been pivotal to the financial crisis. But he did not. In the one and a half pages of the 700-page book devoted to this specific topic, Piketty acknowledges the contribution of inequality to the financial crisis of 2008 but concludes that "it was not the sole or even primary cause" (p. 298).

Relations of personal dependence (entirely spontaneous at the outset) are the first social forms, in which human productive capacity develops to a slight extent and at isolated points. Personal independence founded on objective dependence is the second great form, in which a system of general metabolism, of universal relations, of all-round needs and universal capacities is formed for the first time. Free individuality, based on the universal development of individuals and on their subordination of their communal, social productivity as their social wealth, is the third stage. The second stage creates the conditions for the third.

(Karl Marx, Grundrisse, 1857)

Appendix A

The figures and table in this appendix give visual indication of the date at which the global commodity system became an operational totality and of the dominant position of the US at the core of that system. In 1980, the aggregate nominal value of world securities stocks was more or less on a par with nominal world GDP for that year. At no time prior to that date was the aggregate value of world securities stocks as great as that of world GDP, while, as can be seen in Figure A.1, at no time since that date has the growth rate of world GDP kept up with the rate of growth of world securities stocks. The commoditisation of financial securities, which marks the completion of a global commodity system, has been key to their huge growth in volume because this growth could only become possible at the point when securities exist as stand-alone stores of value that can be traded away from their initial conditions of issuance, and because that point can only be reached when there are in place globally uniform benchmarks against which the risks on securities can be monitored and controlled from a distance. If the US' position as the world's leading supplier of securities exceeds its position as one of the world's major suppliers of material outputs, as shown in Table A.1, this is because, as explained in the text, the US is unique in its ability to combine a production base of sufficient size and a governance infrastructure of sufficient strength as to be able to generate and maintain vast securities stocks. Figure A.2, which shows the regional size asymmetries in outstanding securities stocks in currency terms, gives visual depiction of the argument that the huge mass of dollar-denominated securities explains not only the dollar's hegemonic position as the currency of choice in an international capacity but also the dollar's gravitational pull on the overwhelming majority of other national currencies. Ultimately, the whole point of understanding that financial securities now have

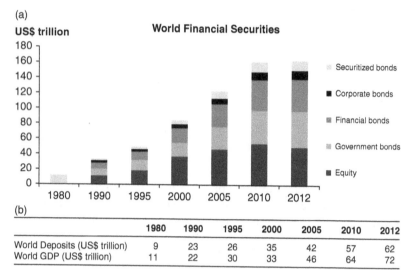

Source: Mckinsey (2013), IMF (2013)

Figure A.1 Growth of securities markets during 1980–2012.
Source: Karltenbrunner and Lysandrou (2107).

Table A.1 Country shares of world GDP, securities stocks and currency market activity, 2012

	US	Eurozone	Japan	UK	China	EMEs (ex. China)
% share of world GDP	22.42	16.83	8.23	3.41	11.36	20.72
% share of world trade	10.74	24.62	4.35	3.60	9.94	27.29
Net trade (US$ billion)	−58	31	−14	−9.8	17	7.6
Exports (US$ billion)	217	581	93	78	226	631
Imports (US$ billion)	276	551	107	88	210	623
% share of world securities (total)	37.49	19.58	12.72	6.13	5.21	
Equities	35.11	11.87	6.92	5.68	6.95	19.52
Bonds	38.88	24.11	16.12	6.39	4.18	N/A
% Share of world currency use	56.92	33.75	8.74	8.56	1.31	8.94

Source: Karltenbrunner and Lysandrou (2017).

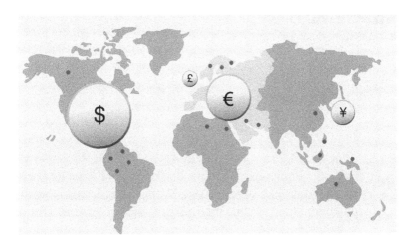

Figure A.2 Major securities markets in currency terms, 2012.

a stock (store of value) dimension as much as a flow (yield) dimension is to understand this gravitational pull of the dollar: because the global stocks of dollar-denominated stores of value dwarf any other currency-denominated stocks, the world's investors have no choice but to hold substantial proportions of their wealth in dollar securities, and it is this absence of choice that helps to explain why so many national currencies are pulled into the dollar's orbit. The distinction between the flow and stock dimensions of securities is especially significant in the case of bonds, a category where the US' position as the world's leading supplier is most prominent: view bonds as only debt instruments on which interests must be paid, and the power of the dollar and the ensuing power of the US' ruling elites make little sense, but view bonds also as secure stores of value, and that power makes complete sense.

Appendix B

The 15 figures presented in this appendix give some visual support to our contention that the chief motivating forces driving the US and European banking sectors to create extra loan-backed securities in the immediate pre-crisis era were demand pull pressures emanating from investors searching for yield rather than internal supply push factors. As argued in the main text, although several of these latter factors, such as the banks' quest for fees and commissions or their exploitation of profit-enhancing arbitrage opportunities, played an important role in the pre-crisis growth of the ABS, CDO and ABCP markets, they did not have causal primacy in that growth. To suggest otherwise is to beg the question as to why the US and European banks waited until 2003–4 before suddenly exploding into activity. What were they doing before this time? Were they not aware of the profitable opportunities to be had before suddenly waking up to these opportunities? On the contrary, the close correlation between the sudden steep rise in global investor demand for US bonds (causing a steep drop in bond yields) and the equally sudden steep rise in the supply rates of ABSs, CDOs and ABCP points to the primacy of investor demand pull pressures behind these supply rates.

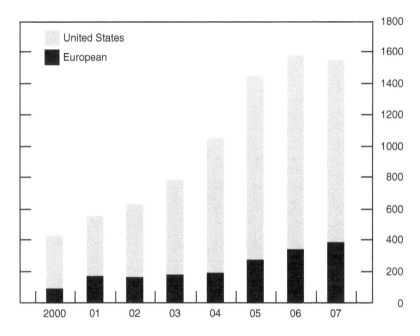

Figure B.1 Asset-backed securities issuance (US$ billion).
Source: Bank of England (2007a).

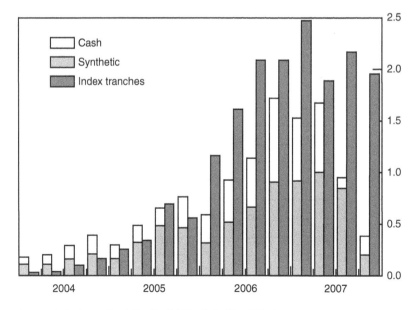

Figure B.2 Growth of CDOs (2003–6) (US$ trillion).
Source: BIS (2007).

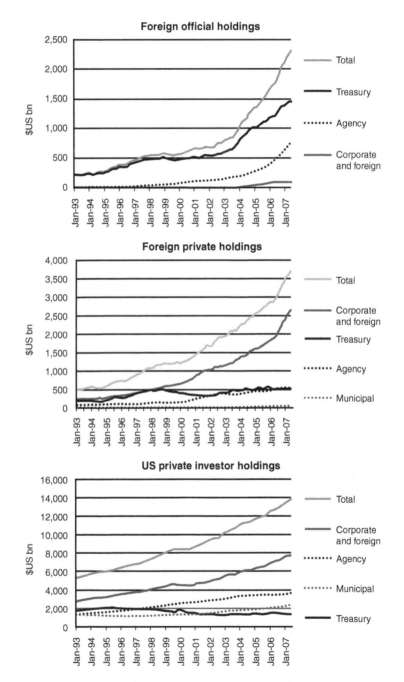

Figure B.3 Foreign and domestic investment in US bond markets (1993–2007).
Source: Goda and Lysandrou (2104).

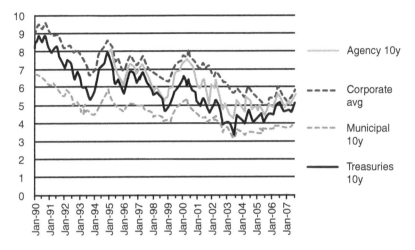

Figure B.4 US bond yields (1990–2007).
Source: Goda and Lysandrou (2014).

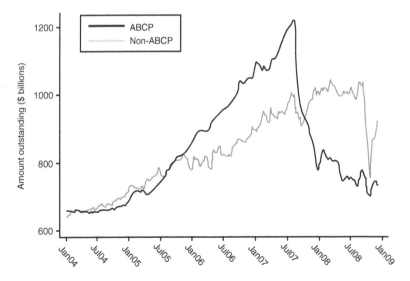

Figure B.5 Commercial paper outstanding (2004–9).
Source: Kacperczyk and Schnabl (2010).

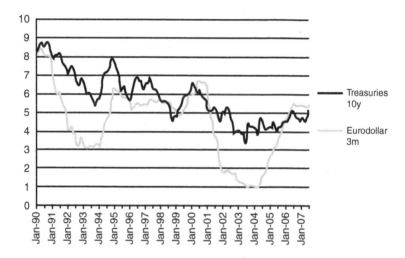

Figure B.6 Long- and short-term interest rates in the US (in %).
Source: Goda and Lysandrou (2014).

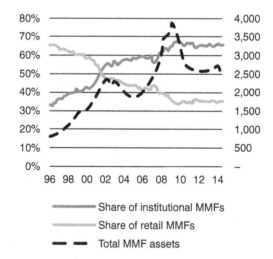

Figure B.7 Assets in US$ billion (right scale) and share in total assets in %
(left scale).
Source: Deutsche Bank (2015).

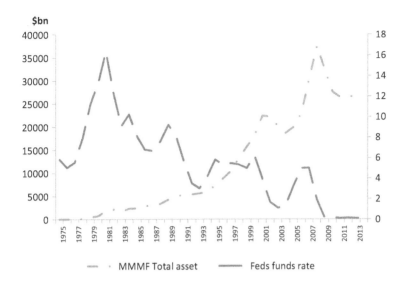

Figure B.8 MMMF assets (left scale) and Feds fund rate (right scale).
Source: Lysandrou and Shabani (2018).

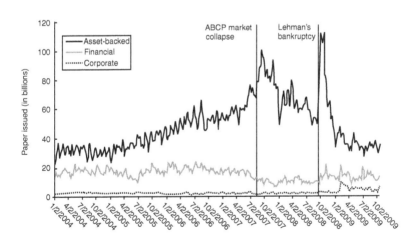

Figure B.9 Commercial paper issuances, January 2004–October 2009.
Source: Kacperczyk and Schnabl (2010).

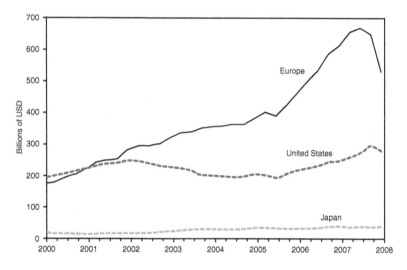

Figure B.10 Global ABCP outstanding by region.
Source: Arteta et al. (2013).

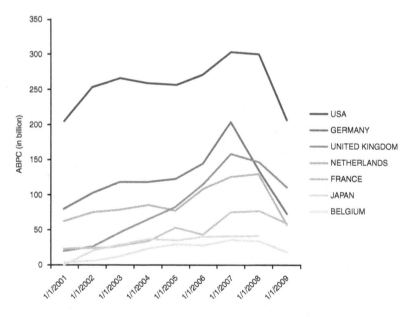

Figure B.11 Growth in bank-sponsored ABCP by country.
Source: Acharya and Schnabl (2010).

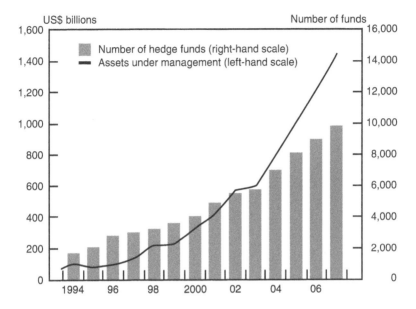

Figure B.12 Number of hedge funds and assets under management.
Source: Lysandrou (2012).

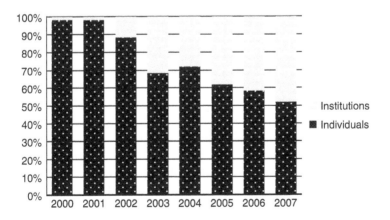

Figure B.13 Source of hedge fund capital by share of assets under management.
Source: Goda and Lysandrou (2014).

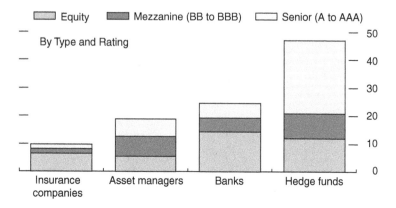

Figure B.14 Buyers of CDOs: 2006 (in percent).
Source: IMF (2008), Lysandrou (2012).

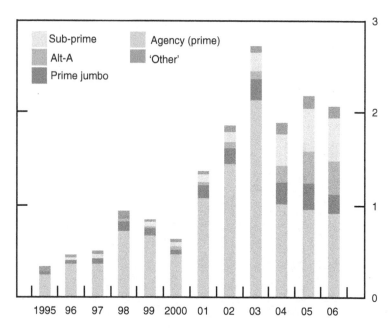

Figure B.15 US residential mortgage-backed securities issuance (US$ trillion).
Source: Bank of England (2007b).

Bibliography

Acharya, VV and Schnabl, P (2010), Do Global Banks Spread Global Imbalances? The Case of ABCP during the Financial Crisis of 2007–09, *IMF Economic Review*, Vol. 58. No. 1, pp. 37–73.

Ahern, J (2007), ABC's of ABCP, Societe Generale.

Arteta, C, Carey, M, Correa, R and Kotter, J (2013), *Revenge of the Steamroller: ABCP as a Window on Risk Choices, Board of Governors of the Federal Reserve System*. International Finance Discussion Papers, No. 1076.

Bank of England (2007a), Financial Stability Report, April.

Bank of England (2007b), Financial Stability Report, October.

Borio, C (2008), *The Financial Turmoil of 2007–?: A Preliminary Assessment and Some Policy Considerations*. BIS Working Papers No. 251, March.

Borio, C (2014), *The International Monetary and Financial System: Its Achilles Heel and What to Do About It*. Bank for International Settlements Working Paper No. 456.

Caballero, R (2010), *The 'Other' Imbalance and the Financial Crisis*. NBER Working Paper, No. 15636.

Capgemini (2016), World Wealth Report.

Deutsche Bank (2015), Money Market Funds – An Economic Perspective, February.

Forbes, KJ (2010), Why Do Foreigners Invest in the United States, *Journal of International Economics*, Vol. 80, No. 1, pp. 3–21.

Goda, T, Lysandrou, P and Stewart, C (2013), The Contribution of US Bond Demand to the US Bond Yield Conundrum of 2004–8: An Empirical Investigation, *Journal of International Money, Finance and Markets*, Vol. 27, No. 2, pp. 113–136.

Goda, T and Lysandrou, P (2014), The Contribution of Wealth Concentration to the Subprime Crisis: A Quantitative Estimation, *Cambridge Journal of Economics*, Vol. 38, No. 2, pp. 301–327.

Godley, W and Lavoie, M (2012), *Monetary Economics* (2nd ed.). London, England: Palgrave.

Grahl, J and Lysandrou, P (2003), Sand in the Wheels or Spanner in the Works: Global Finance and the Tobin Tax, *Cambridge Journal of Economics*, Vol. 27, No. 4, pp. 597–621.

Grahl, J and Lysandrou, P (2006) Capital Market Trading Volume: An Overview and Some Preliminary Conclusions, *Cambridge Journal of Economics*, Vol. 30, No. 6, pp. 955–979.

Grahl, J and Lysandrou, P (2014), The European Commission's Proposal for a Financial Transactions Tax: A Critical Appraisal, *Journal of Common Market Studies*, Vol. 52, No. 2, pp. 234–249.

Hall, PA and Soskice, D (2001), *Varieties of Capitalism*. Basingstoke, England: Oxford University Press.

International Monetary Fund (2008), Global Financial Stability Report, July.

Kacperczyk, M and Schnabl, P (2010), When Safe Proved Risky: Commercial Paper during the Financial Crisis of 2007–2009, *Journal of Economic Perspectives*, Vol. 24, No. 1, pp. 29–50.

Karabarbounis, L and Neiman, B (2013), *The Global Decline of the Labour Share*. NBER Working Paper 19136.

Karltenbrunner, A and Lysandrou, P (2017), The US Dollar's Continuing Hegemony as an International Currency: A Double Matrix Analysis, *Development and Change*, Vol. 48, No. 4, pp. 663–691.

Lysandrou, P (1987), "On Marx's Contribution to a Unified Theory of Price." In *British Review of Economic Issues*, Vol. 9, No. 21, pp. 65–89, Reprinted in Blaug, M ed. (1990) *Karl Marx*, Aldershot: Edward Elgar.

Lysandrou, P (1996), Methodological Dualism and the Microfoundations of Marx's Economic Theory, *Cambridge Journal of Economics*, Vol. 20, No. 5, pp. 565–584.

Lysandrou, P (2000), The Market and Exploitation in Marx's Economic Theory: A Re-interpretation, *Cambridge Journal of Economics*, Vol. 24, No. 3, pp. 325–347.

Lysandrou, P (2005), Globalisation as Commodification, *Cambridge Journal of Economics*, Vol. 29, No. 5, pp. 769–797.

Lysandrou, P (2011a), Global Inequality, Wealth Concentration and the Subprime Crisis: A Marxian Commodity Theory Analysis, *Development and Change*, Vol. 42, No. 1, pp. 183–208

Lysandrou, P (2011b), Global inequality as One of the Root Causes of the Financial Crisis: A Suggested Interpretation, *Economy and Society*, Vol. 40, No. 3, pp. 323–344.

Lysandrou, P (2011c), The Primacy of Hedge Funds in the Subprime Crisis, *Journal of Post Keynesian Economics*, Vol. 34, No. 2, pp. 225–254.

Lysandrou, P (2013a), Debt Intolerance and the 90% Debt Threshold: Two Impossibility Theorems, *Economy and Society*, Vol. 42, No. 4, pp. 521–542.

Lysandrou, P (2013b), The New Rationale for Corporate Limited Liability, *International Journal of Public Policy*, Vol. 9, No. 3, pp. 215–230.

Lysandrou, P (2014), Post-Keynesian Stock-Flow Models after the Sub-prime Crisis: The Need for Microfoundations, *European Journal of Economics and Economic Policy*, Vol. 11, No. 1, pp. 113–126.

Lysandrou, P (2016), The Colonisation of the Future: An Alternative View of Financialisation and Its Portents, *Journal of Post-Keynesian Economics*, Vol. 39, No. 4, pp. 444–472.

Lysandrou, P and Lysandrou, Y (2003), Global English and Proregression: Understanding English Language Spread in the Contemporary Era, *Economy and Society*, Vol. 32, No. 2, pp. 207–233.

Lysandrou, P and Stoyanova, D (2007), The Anachronism of the Voice Exit Paradigm: Institutional Investors and UK Corporate Governance, *Corporate Governance: International Review*, Vol. 15, No. 6, pp. 1070–1078.

Lysandrou, P and Ada Pra, F (2010), The Irrelevance of the European Union's Takeover Directive, *Competition and Change*, Vol. 14, Nos 3–4, pp. 203–220.

Lysandrou, P and Parker, D (2012), Commercial Corporate Governance Ratings: An Alternative View of their Use and Impact, *International Review of Applied Economics*, Vol. 26, No. 4, pp. 445–463.

Lysandrou, P and Nesvetailova, A (2015), The Role of Shadow Bank Entities in the Sub-prime Crisis: A Disaggregated View, *Review of International Political Economy*, Vol. 22, No. 2, pp. 257–279.

Lysandrou, P and Shabani, M (2018), The Explosive Growth of the ABCP Market between 2004 and 2007: A 'Search for Yield' Story, *Journal of Post-Keynesian Economics*, forthcoming.

Marx, K (1976), "Notes on Wagner." In *Value: Studies By Karl Marx*, edited by Dragstedt A, 195–229. Clapham, London: New Park Publications.

Merton, RC and Brodie, Z (1995), "A Conceptual Framework for Analyzing the Financial Environment." In *The Global Financial System: A Functional Perspective*, edited by Crane D, 3–12. Boston, MA: Harvard Business School.

Piketty, T (2014), *Capital in the Twenty First Century*. Cambridge, MA: Harvard University Press.

Rajan, R (2010), *Fault Lines: How Hidden Fractures Still Threaten the World Economy*. Princeton, Woodstock: Princeton University Press.

Reinhart, C and Rogoff, K (2009), *This Time Is Different: Eight Centuries of Financial Folly*. Princeton, Woodstock: Princeton University Press.

Reinhart, C and Rogoff, K (2010). *Growth in a Time of Debt*. NBER Working Paper 15639.

Stone, I (1999), *The Global Export of Capital from Great Britain, 1865–1914*. Basingstoke and London: Macmillan Press.

Wallerstein, I (1974), *The Modern World-System: Capitalist Agriculture and the Origins of the European World-Economy in the Sixteenth Century*. New York: Academic Press.

Index